USING
itunes® 10

Nancy Conner

800 East 96th Street, Indianapolis, Indiana 46240 USA

Using iTunes® 10

Copyright © 2011 by Pearson Education, Inc.

ISBN-13: 978-0-7897-4787-7

ISBN-10: 0-7897-4787-1

Library of Congress Cataloging-in-Publication Data is on file.

Printed in the United States of America

First Printing: February 2011

Trademarks

Warning and Disclaimer

Bulk Sales

Que Publishing offers excellent discounts on this book when ordered in quantity for bulk purchases or special sales. For more information, please contact

U.S. Corporate and Government Sales
1-800-382-3419
corpsales@pearsontechgroup.com
For sales outside of the U.S., please contact

International Sales
international@pearson.com

Associate Publisher
Greg Wiegand

Acquisitions Editor
Laura Norman

Development Editor
Dan Workman

Managing Editor
Kristy Hart

Project Editor
Betsy Harris

Copy Editor
Krista Hansing Editorial Services

Senior Indexer
Cheryl Lenser

Proofreader
Paula Lowell

Technical Editor
Christian Kenyeres

Publishing Coordinator
Cindy Teeters

Interior Designer
Anne Jones

Cover Designer
Anna Stingley

Multimedia Developer
John Herrin

Senior Compositor
Gloria Schurick

Contents at a Glance

Media Table of Contents

To register this product and gain access to the Free Web Edition and the audio and video files, go to **quepublishing.com/using**.

Table of Contents

About the Author

Nancy Conner has written more than a dozen technical and reference books on topics ranging from eBay to Microsoft Office, from classical mythology to Google Apps, from green living to Zoho. Nancy holds a Ph.D. from Brown University and has worked as a medievalist, high-school teacher, editor, and corporate trainer. She lives in upstate New York with her husband, Steven Holzner, where they both work from home without getting on each other's nerves. When she's not writing, she enjoys reading fantasy novels, visiting local wineries, and listening obsessively to opera.

Dedication

To Steve. You're the best, and I'm the luckiest.

Acknowledgments

Writing a book is a team effort, and I appreciate all the people who made this book possible. Thank you Laura Norman, acquisition editor; Dan Workman, development editor; and Betsy Harris, production editor. I'm also grateful to my copy editor, Krista Hansing; my technical editor, Christian Kenyeres; and my proofreader, Paula Lowell. I owe thanks, as always, to my agent, Carole Jelen. Thanks to Tamsen Conner for Mac support. And special thanks to my husband, Steven Holzner, for his constant love and support.

We Want to Hear from You!

As the reader of this book, *you* are our most important critic and commentator. We value your opinion and want to know what we're doing right, what we could do better, what areas you'd like to see us publish in, and any other words of wisdom you're willing to pass our way.

As an associate publisher for Que Publishing, I welcome your comments. You can email or write me directly to let me know what you did or didn't like about this book—as well as what we can do to make our books better.

Please note that I cannot help you with technical problems related to the topic of this book. We do have a User Services group, however, where I will forward specific technical questions related to the book.

When you write, please be sure to include this book's title and author, as well as your name, email address, and phone number. I will carefully review your comments and share them with the author and editors who worked on the book.

Email: feedback@quepublishing.com
Mail: Greg Wiegand
             Associate Publisher
             Que Publishing
             800 East 96th Street
             Indianapolis, IN 46240 USA

Reader Services

Visit our website and register this book at quepublishing.com/register for convenient access to any updates, downloads, or errata that might be available for this book.

Introduction

For 10 years, iTunes has brought listening pleasure to people's computers. Originally introduced in January 2001, the first version of iTunes worked only with Mac OS 9 operating systems, but later that year, Apple added support for OS X and for iPods—and that's when iTunes really took off. Subsequent versions of the software included the addition of the iTunes Store, support for Microsoft Windows, and cool features like Cover Flow view, which lets you browse your album covers as though you were flipping through a rack of CDs, and Genius playlists, which analyze your preferences to create great-sounding music mixes.

With iTunes 10, Apple has done it again. For one thing, Apple has declared the victory of digital music over physical CDs by removing the background CD from the iTunes logo. But that's just window-dressing. There are also TV show rentals; Air Play, which lets you stream music wirelessly to external speakers; improved syncing; and a new version of Apple TV. But the real innovation in iTunes 10 is Ping, which brings music-oriented social networking into iTunes. Ping lets you connect with friends and your favorite artists—sharing recommendations and reviews, following news, finding local events, and more. It's a great way to connect with others through your common interest: music.

Whether you're new to iTunes or have been using it for years, this book gets you up to speed—fast—with getting the most out of iTunes.

How This Book Is Organized

This book introduces you to iTunes 10 and shows you how to get the most out of it. You'll learn what to expect from iTunes 10 and what the program limitations are, as well as best practices for using iTunes. *Using iTunes 10* teaches you how to download and enjoy music, videos, and more; how to organize your iTunes library; and how to use the new social networking options Apple has integrated with iTunes 10. Here's what you'll find in *Using iTunes 10*:

- Getting started with iTunes 10

- Adding music, videos, and other content into your iTunes library

- Syncing your iPod, iPhone, or iPad with iTunes to keep your devices up-to-date

- Creating playlists and organizing the contents of your iTunes library

- Sharing your music and videos over a home network

- Using Ping, iTunes' new built-in social network for music lovers

- Getting familiar with key concepts, especially for novice users

- Learning tips and tricks for getting the most out of iTunes

Using This Book

This book allows you to customize your own learning experience. The step-by-step instructions in the book give you a solid foundation in using iTunes 10, while content, including video tutorials and audio sidebars, provides the following:

- Demonstrations of step-by-step tasks covered in the book

- Additional tips or information on a topic

- Practical advice and suggestions

- Direction for more advanced tasks not covered in the book

Here's a quick look at a few structural features designed to help you get the most out of this book.

- **Chapter objective:** At the beginning of each chapter is a brief summary of topics addressed in that chapter. This objective enables you to quickly see what the chapter covers.

Notes provide additional commentary or explanation that doesn't fit neatly into the surrounding text. Notes give detailed explanations of how something works, alternative ways of performing a task, and other tidbits to get you on your way.

☺ *Cross-references: Many topics are connected to other topics in various ways. Cross-references help you link related information, no matter where that information appears in the book. When another section is related to one you are reading, a cross-reference directs you to a specific page in the book where you can find the related information.*

LET ME TRY IT tasks are presented in a step-by-step sequence so you can easily follow along.

 SHOW ME video walks through tasks you just have to see—including bonus advanced techniques.

 TELL ME MORE audio delivers practical insights straight from the experts.

Special Features

More than just a book, your USING product integrates step-by-step video tutorials and valuable audio sidebars delivered through the **Free Web Edition** that comes with every USING book. For the price of the book, you get online access anywhere with a web connection—no books to carry, content is updated as the technology changes, and the benefit of video and audio learning.

About the USING Web Edition

The Web Edition of every USING book is powered by **Safari Books Online**, allowing you to access the video tutorials and valuable audio sidebars. Plus, you can search the contents of the book, highlight text and attach a note to that text, print your notes and highlights in a custom summary, and cut and paste directly from Safari Books Online.

To register this product and gain access to the Free Web Edition and the audio and video files, go to **quepublishing.com/using**.

This chapter gets you up to speed with iTunes 10. You'll learn how to install iTunes, get familiar with the iTunes window, and set up your iPod, iPhone, or iPad.

1

Getting Started with iTunes 10

Welcome to iTunes 10! If you're looking for a way to easily store, organize, and play media files, you've come to the right place. iTunes is an audio player, a video player, a complete media library, and more.

This chapter serves as your introduction to iTunes 10, complete with guided tour. After a quick overview of what you can do with iTunes, you'll learn how to download and install the program to your computer. Next, you'll see what's where in the main iTunes window. See how to customize the window, sort tracks, view your collection, and make iTunes your default player.

You don't *have* to have an iPod to enjoy iTunes, but if you want to take your tunes, movies, and videos with you when you're on the go, an iPod is the easiest way to do it. (That includes the iPod that comes with an iPhone or iPad.) The chapter ends by showing you how to get your iPod in sync with iTunes.

What Can You Do with iTunes?

iTunes is a system for organizing and playing your media files. You can use iTunes to set up a library to store your albums, music videos, movies, and TV shows; listen to music; watch videos; and transfer files to your portable media device. Whether you're brand-new to iTunes or you've been using it for a while, you'll appreciate these benefits:

- Rip songs from your CDs and store them on your computer. (Sounds painful, but it won't hurt your CDs a bit.) You can also burn CDs—copy music from your computer to a disc—to back up your collection.

- Listen to music through your computer. When you put a CD into your computer's CD/DVD drive, you can listen to it in iTunes. But there are lots of ways to listen to music using iTunes: You can get music by downloading it from the Internet or buying it in the iTunes Store, and then listen to it immediately in iTunes. You can also listen to Internet radio.

- Fine-tune your playback so your music sounds its best.

- Create playlists so you can put together your favorite songs in the order you like to hear them. The iTunes Genius feature will even search your library and put together great-sounding playlists for you.

Ⓖ *Chapter 5, "Playing with Playlists," is all about creating and listening to playlists.*

- Watch videos. iTunes has a built-in video player, so you can watch your favorite videos on your computer. You can also upload videos to your portable media player or (if you have Apple TV) watch them on your television.

- Listen to podcasts. Whether you subscribe to a podcast or just listen to an occasional episode, you can do that through iTunes.

- Listen to audiobooks. Lots of people enjoy listening to audiobooks on the daily commute or just to relax. Tune in to iTunes to keep up with your favorite authors without getting eyestrain.

Ⓖ *If you have an iPod Touch, iPhone, or iPad, you can also get iBooks (Apple's version of eBooks) through the App Store.* **See** *"iTunes and iBooks," (in Chapter 6, "Viewing in iTunes: TV, Movies, and More") to learn how.*

- Organize your media files, making it easy to find whatever song or video you're in the mood for when you're in the mood for it.

- Keep your computer's media library and your iPod, iPhone, or iPad, in sync.

- Share your favorites over a network or, through Home Sharing, with up to five authorized computers in your home. And because Apple knows it's nice to share, you can also use Ping, the social network that's new in iTunes 10, to share your latest and greatest discoveries with your friends.

- See what your favorite artists are up to by following them on Ping. You can also locate concerts near you and find out what your friends are listening to.

This book covers all these topics and more, to help you get the most out of iTunes. So let's get started by seeing how you can get iTunes.

 TELL ME MORE   Media 1.1—What's New in iTunes 10?
Access this audio recording through your registered Web Edition at **my.safaribooksonline.com/9780132660273/media**.

Who Can Use iTunes?

The iTunes software is free—you don't have to spend a dime to download and install it. (So you can save your money for when you decide to go shopping in the iTunes Store.)

ⓖ *To learn about buying music, videos, and more in the iTunes Store,* **see** *Chapter 3, "Shopping in the iTunes Store."*

To get iTunes 10, you need a computer that runs Mac OS X or Windows, and an Internet connection. Read on to learn the system requirements for using iTunes 10.

What about other operating systems? Sorry, no go. iTunes doesn't support Linux Ubuntu, Google Chrome OS, or any operating system besides those listed in this section.

If You Use a Macintosh

If your computer is a Mac, make sure it meets these system requirements so you can install iTunes 10:

- **Processor**—Intel, PowerPC G5 or G4 processor.

- **Memory**—At least 512MB of RAM. (If you want to play to play HD video, an iTunes LP, or iTunes Extras, you'll need 1GB.)

- **Available disk space**—At least 200MB.

- **Operating system**—Mac OS X version 10.5 or later.

- **Multimedia player**—QuickTime 7.6 or later.

- **Video RAM**—At least 16MB so you can watch videos.

- **CD/DVD recorder**—Apple combo drive or SuperDrive to create audio, MP3, or back-up CDs. (If you want to back up your library to DVDs, you'll need SuperDrive.) Some non-Apple recorders may work, as long as they're compatible with iTunes.

- **Web browser**—Safari 4.0.3 or later.

If your Mac is an older G3 model, iTunes 10 won't work with your computer. The most recent version of iTunes for G3 Macs is iTunes 8.2.1. You can download it at http://support.apple.com/kb/DL857.

If You Use a PC

For PC folks, here's a list of system requirements for using iTunes 10:

- **Processor**—Intel or AMD processor of at least 1GHz. (If you plan to play HD video, an iTunes LP, or iTunes Extras from the iTunes Store, you need a 2.0GHz Intel Core 2 Duo—or faster—processor.)

- **Memory**—At least 512MB of RAM (1GB if you want to play HD video, an iTunes LP, or iTunes Extras).

- **Available disk space**—At least 200MB.

- **Operating system**—Windows XP (Service Pack 2 or later), Windows Vista (32-bit edition), or Windows 7 (32-bit edition). If you have a 64-bit version of Vista or Windows 7, go to http://support.apple.com/kb/DL1047 to download the iTunes 64-bit installer.

- **Multimedia player**—QuickTime 7.6.6 or later (included in the iTunes download). Make sure your computer has a QuickTime-compatible audio card.

- **Audio card**—Must be compatible with QuickTime.

- **Video card**—Must be compatible with DirectX 9.0–compatible video card and have at least 32MB of video RAM (64MB is better).

- **CD/DVD recorder**—So you can create backups of your iTunes library.

Requirements for Everyone

Whether you use Windows or a Mac, keep these further requirements in mind:

- **Screen resolution**—Set your monitor's screen resolution to 1,024x768 or greater. iTunes LPs and iTunes Extras work best with a screen resolution of 1,280x800 or greater.

- **Broadband Internet connection**—You'll need a high-speed connection to the Internet to use the iTunes Store.

- **Available disk space**—iTunes requires 200MB to install.

Getting iTunes

When you're ready to install iTunes on your computer, point your web browser to www.apple.com/itunes and click the big blue Download iTunes button. On the page that opens, click Download Now and follow the steps to download the iTunes setup program to your computer. (These steps vary, depending on your web browser and whether you have a Mac or a Windows-based PC.)

If you're already using a previous version of iTunes to sync various devices, such as an iPod and your iPhone, be sure to do a full sync of all those devices before you install iTunes 10.

ⓖ *Not sure how to sync your devices?* **See** *"Syncing Your iPod, iPhone, or iPad with iTunes" (in Chapter 9, "Syncing and Sharing").*

Finding Your Way Around

The Windows and Mac versions of iTunes are very similar, as Figures 1.1 and 1.2 show. In Windows (see Figure 1.1), iTunes has an upper-left row of menu commands—File, Edit, View, and so on—that you won't see in the iTunes window on your Macintosh (see Figure 1.2). Instead, menu commands appear in the Active Application bar at the very top of a Mac's screen. (When Windows and Mac use different command names, this book gives both.) Differences also show up in the appearance of dialog boxes and icons, because of differences in the Windows and Mac OS X operating systems. But even though dialog boxes look different, their contents are the same.

SHOW ME   Media 1.2—Finding Your Way Around
Access this video file through your registered Web Edition at
my.safaribooksonline.com/9780132660273/media.

Mac users may wonder what happened to their Close, Minimize, and Maximize buttons. In iTunes 10, these buttons are vertical instead of the horizontal arrangement you may be used to seeing.

As you can see in Figures 1.1 and 1.2, the main iTunes window is pretty straightforward. It has these main elements:

- **Controls bar**—The bar across the top of the iTunes window, shown in Figure 1.3, contains these controls:

  - **Menu commands**—In Windows, go to the upper-left corner when you want to work with iTunes: add new files, create a playlist, set preferences, turn on sharing, and so on.

If you use iTunes on a Mac, the iTunes menu commands appear at the very top of your screen, in the Active Application bar.

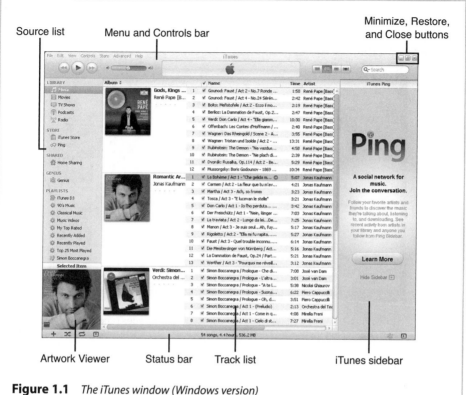

Figure 1.1   *The iTunes window (Windows version)*

- **iTunes player**—Start or pause playback, switch to a different track, or adjust the volume.

- **Status pane**—The Status pane tells you what iTunes is doing right now. Look here to see information about the track that's currently playing. If nothing is loaded in the player, you see the Apple logo. If you're shopping in the iTunes Store, this pane lets you know when a page in the store is loading or shows your progress in downloading a purchase. When iTunes syncs with your iPod, the Status pane tells you that's happening, too.

- **View buttons**—These buttons change how your tracks display in the main part of the iTunes window. (See "Different Ways of Viewing Your Music," coming up later in this chapter, to explore your view options.)

- **Search box**—Here's where you can search for a specific track in your library.

- **Track list**—The middle of the window shows your library's tracks. Double-click any song to play it.

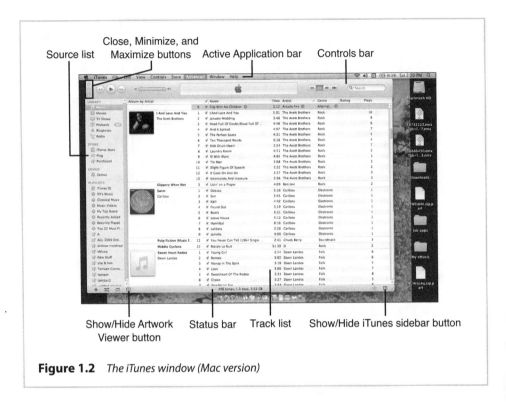

Source list   Close, Minimize, and   Active Application bar   Controls bar
                Maximize buttons

Show/Hide Artwork   Status bar   Track list   Show/Hide iTunes sidebar button
Viewer button

Figure 1.2 *The iTunes window (Mac version)*

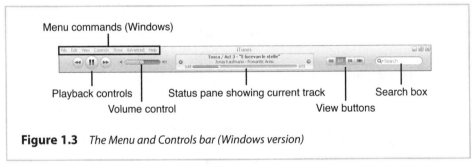

Menu commands (Windows)

Playback controls   Status pane showing current track   Search box
Volume control   View buttons

Figure 1.3 *The Menu and Controls bar (Windows version)*

ⓒ *For step-by-step instructions on listening to music from your iTunes library, **see** "Listening to Music in Your iTunes Library" (in Chapter 4, "Listening in iTunes").*

- **Source list**—If you want to switch from, say, listening to music to watching a video, use this pane to access different parts of your iTunes library. Click iTunes Store to go shopping or Ping to interact with your friends. You can also work with home sharing and playlists by clicking the relevant links in this pane.

ⓖ *For information about the iTunes Store,* **see** *Chapter 3. Chapter 10, "Ping: iTunes Goes Social," tells you all about Ping. Get the scoop on home sharing in Chapter 9 and on working with playlists in Chapter 5.*

- **Artwork Viewer**—Here you can display the cover art of the album you're listening to now.

To show or hide album art in the Artwork Viewer, click the Show/Hide button just beneath it—it's the fourth button from the left on the status bar.

- **Status bar**—Stretching across the bottom of the window, as shown in Figure 1.4, this bar has playlist and shuffle controls on the left side, and a button that lets you show or hide the iTunes sidebar on the right side. In the middle, you get information about the size of your current library. For example, if you're in your Music library, you'll see how many songs that library holds, how much total playing time they add up to, and how much space they take up on your computer.

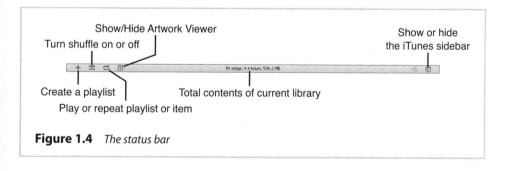

Figure 1.4   *The status bar*

- **Show/Hide iTunes sidebar button**—The iTunes sidebar combines the best of Genius and Ping: Genius analyzes your iTunes library and recommends music you might like and, Ping, the social network for music lovers that's new in iTunes 10, lets you keep an eye on what your favorite artists and friends are doing.

If the iTunes sidebar takes up too much room, hide it by clicking its Hide Sidebar button or the Show/Hide button just below it on the status bar.

Customizing Your iTunes Window

Your default iTunes window looks something like the ones shown in Figures 1.1 and 1.2. But you can tweak the way iTunes looks to suit your preferences. The columns in your track list, for example, are customizable, and you can decide which ones you want to show or hide. iTunes also offers different ways to view your collection; pick the one you like best or switch between them. This section tells you how to do all that and more.

Showing Only the Info You Want to See

Your iTunes track list shows columns that give information about each track. By default, you'll see the name, time, artist, genre, and so on for each track. But you can customize the information you see in your track list. To do that, select View, View Options, or press Ctrl+J (Cmd-J on a Mac). This opens the View Options dialog box shown in Figure 1.5.

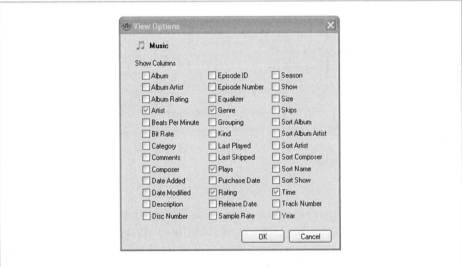

Figure 1.5   *The View Options dialog box*

If you're looking at your music collection in Grid view, which doesn't list individual album tracks, View Options is unavailable.

Each item in the View Options dialog box represents a column in your track list. If you wanted to see the date you added each track, for example, you'd put a checkmark in the Date Added check box. If you didn't want to display the Genre column, you'd remove the checkmark from that check box.

> The changes you make in View Options apply only to the columns for the group you've selected. In other groups, the columns are not affected.

After you've made your selections, click OK to change the columns in your track list.

> Here's a quick way to show or hide a single column: Right-click (Ctrl-click on a Mac) any column heading. iTunes shows a menu of all possible column headings. Click the name of any column to select (or deselect) it.

Resizing Columns

If a column is too narrow—it cuts off the full names of albums or artists, for example—you can resize it. To resize a single column, go to the header bar and hover your mouse pointer over the vertical line that marks the boundary between the column you want to resize and its neighbor. (You'll know you're in the right spot when the pointer changes to a thick vertical bar with horizontal arrows pointing out from it.) Click and drag to make the column smaller or larger. The column resizes as you drag; when it's the width you want, let go of the mouse button.

You can also autosize columns. This means that iTunes adjusts the column width so you can read all entries—nothing gets truncated. To autosize, right-click (Ctrl-click on a Mac) any column header and choose one of these options from the context menu:

- **Autosize Column**—Autosizes only the column whose header you clicked.

- **Autosize All Columns**—Adjusts the widths of all the columns displayed in your track list.

Different Ways of Viewing Your Music

It's your music library, and you can view its contents the way you like. iTunes offers four different ways to look at the contents of your library:

- **List view**—This view, shown in Figure 1.6, hides the Album column, showing your tracks as a list.

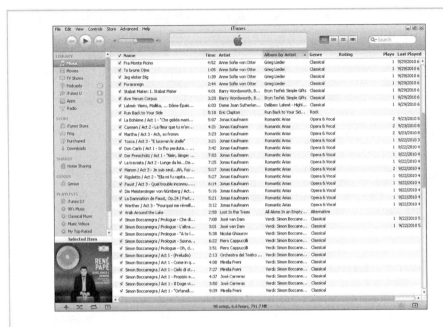

Figure 1.6   *List view*

- **Album List view**—This view looks like the iTunes windows shown in Figures 1.1 and 1.2. The left Album column identifies which album tracks belong to, displaying the cover art if it's available.

  ⓖ *To learn how to get the cover art for tracks you rip from a CD,* **see** *"Adding Cover Art" (in Chapter 2, "Getting Content into iTunes").*

- **Grid view**—This shows your music in a grid, displaying the cover art (if available) for each song. As the next section ("Sorting Content") explains, Grid view lets you group and sort your music by album, artist, genre, or composer. Figure 1.7 shows an example of Grid view.

- **Cover Flow view**—The coolest iTunes view is a 3D, animated display of your album covers, as shown in Figure 1.8. Find the album you want by flipping through the covers. Click the cover you want to see, and the track list changes to display its songs.

 SHOW ME   Media 1.3—Views in iTunes
Access this video file through your registered Web Edition at
my.safaribooksonline.com/9780132660273/media.

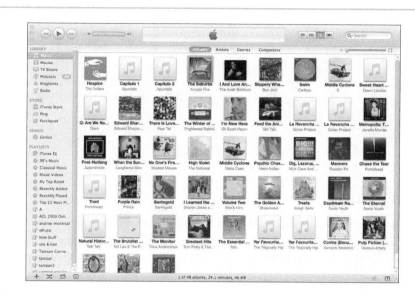

Figure 1.7   *Grid view*

Figure 1.8   *Cover Flow view*

If your computer runs Windows XP and the iTunes Cover Flow doesn't work for you, try this: Right-click your Desktop and select Properties from the pop-up menu to open the Display Properties dialog box. Click the Settings tab, then click Advanced. In the dialog box that opens, click the Troubleshoot tab. Move the Hardware accelerator slider all the way to the right. Click OK, then click OK again. If you have iTunes open, close it. When you start up iTunes again, Cover Flow should work.

Sorting Content

As your music library grows, you'll want to be able to find the songs you're looking for quickly, with minimum hassle. One fast, easy way to find and play your songs is to sort your track list. You have different options for sorting, depending on what view you're in:

- **List view**—Click any column header above the track list to sort your library by that column. If you're in List view, for example, and you click the Name header, iTunes sorts your songs by individual track name, in alphabetical order. When you sort, an arrow appears next to the header you're sorting by. An upward-pointing arrow means you're sorting in ascending order (A–Z or 1, 2, 3); a downward-pointing arrow means you're sorting in descending order (Z–A or 3,2,1). Click the header again to switch from ascending to descending order, or vice versa.

- **Album List view**—This view adds the Album column to those you see in plain-vanilla List view and groups songs by album. When you click the Album header, iTunes gives you these sorting options:

  - **Album by Title**—Choose this option to sort your albums alphabetically by title.

  - **Album by Artist**—If you have several albums by the same artist and want to see those albums grouped together, choose this option. Within each artist grouping, iTunes lists albums in alphabetical order.

  - **Album by Year**—Want to find songs for your Greatest Disco Hits of the '70s playlist? Use this sort, which groups your albums first by artist and then chronologically by year.

- **Grid view**—Your sorting options in this view appear at the top of the screen, above the grid. Click the option you want to sort alphabetically by album, artist, genre, or composer.

- **Cover Flow view**—The default sort of Cover Flow view is Album by Artist, which makes browsing your albums like sorting through racks of CDs or LPs in an old-fashioned record store. (Remember those?) As with the list views, however, you can click any column header to sort by it. For example, if you want to flip through your collection by genre, click the Genre column header to see your albums grouped that way—first by genre, then alphabetically by artist.

Using the Column Browser

One way to sort the contents of your library is to use the Column Browser, shown in Figure 1.9. Turning on the Column Browser switches your library to List view and adds one or more columns that you can use to zero in on the track you're looking for. You can choose the columns to add for browsing, and you can display at the top of the screen or along the left side.

Figure 1.9 *The Column Browser, with columns displayed at the top of the library*

Here's an example of how the Column Browser works. Say you want to quickly find everything in your library by a particular artist. When you turn on the Column Browser and display the Artists column, you can quickly look through that column and click the name of the artist you want. When you do, your library changes to display only tracks by that artist. If you have dozens of tracks by that artist and you're looking for a particular blues song, you could have the Column Browser display Artist and Genre columns. Select the artist, select Blues—and browse the results to find your track. Using the Column Browser is a good way to sift through the contents of a huge library.

To show the Column Browser, select View, Column Browser. Then, from the flyout menu, select the columns you want to display and whether you want the Column Browser to appear at the side or the top of your iTunes library. You can show or hide the Column Browser by pressing Ctrl+B (on a PC) or Cmd-B (on a Mac) to toggle it on and off.

Making iTunes Your Default Player

When you slip a CD into your CD-ROM drive, your computer reads the disc to determine what kind of files it holds. If the files are audio files, your computer opens a program that can play those files. The program that opens automatically when it's time to play a song is your *default player*.

If you use Windows, the installer asked whether you wanted to make iTunes your default player when you installed iTunes. If you said yes, you're all set. If you said no, however, or you somehow missed that question and you've decided that you want iTunes to be your default player, you can make it the default in just a few quick steps.

iTunes already is the default media player on Macintosh computers. So Mac users can skip this section.

 SHOW ME   Media 1.4—Setting Up iTunes as Your Default Audio Player in Windows
Access this video file through your registered Web Edition at my.safaribooksonline.com/9780132660273/media.

 **LET ME TRY IT**

Making iTunes Your Default Audio Player in Windows

For Windows users, here's how to make sure iTunes opens when you want to play a song:

1. In iTunes, select Edit, Preferences, or use the keyboard shortcut
    Ctrl+comma.

2. In the iTunes dialog box, click the Advanced tab (see Figure 1.10).

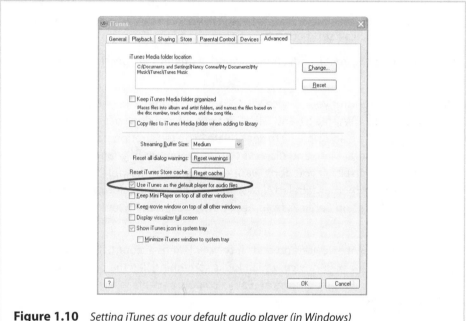

Figure 1.10   *Setting iTunes as your default audio player (in Windows)*

3. Put a checkmark in the check box labeled Use iTunes As the Default Player
    for Audio Files.

4. Click OK.

Setting Up Your iPod, iPhone, or iPad

iTunes is a terrific media organizer and player for your computer—and your computer is all you need to use it. But many people get iTunes because they want to
take their music and videos with them wherever they go. And the easiest way to do
that is with an iPod. You can even use the iPod that comes built into your iPhone or
iPad. Keeping your portable library in sync with your computer's library is as easy
as plugging a cable into a USB port.

To get started, use the USB cable that came with your iPod, iPhone, or iPad to connect to your computer. If this is the first time you've connected the device, your

computer may take a couple of minutes to install its drivers, which allow your iPod and computer to work together. Then iTunes launches automatically (if you haven't opened it already).

You can register your new iPod, iPhone, or iPad with Apple now, if you want, but this step is optional—and if you've already registered your device, perhaps with an earlier version of iTunes, you won't see it. If you don't yet have an account at the iTunes Store, you can set that up, too.

⊙ **See** *"Creating Your iTunes Store Account" in Chapter 3 to get started with the iTunes Store.*

If you want to register your device, click Continue. iTunes asks you to sign in, so do that now, using an Apple ID, and click Continue. (If you don't yet have an Apple ID, click I Do Not Have an Apple ID to set one up.) The registration page asks you to confirm your contact info and displays the serial number of your device (it gets this from the device itself). If you don't want to get email from Apple, remove the checkmark from the box labeled News, Special Offers, and Information About Related Products and Services from Apple. When everything looks good, click Submit.

iTunes registers your device and adds it to your iTunes account. It opens the Summary page for your device, which looks something like the one shown in Figure 1.11. Your iPod (or iPhone or iPad) also now appears in the Devices section of the source list.

At the bottom of your Summary page, the capacity bar shows how much space is available on your device, as well as how much space different kinds of files—audio, photos, apps, books, and other—are taking up.

iTunes also automatically syncs the libraries of your computer and your iPod, so you always have all your songs (and other media files) handy, no matter where you're listening to them.

Don't disconnect your iPod or other device from your computer while it's syncing with iTunes. Wait until you see the message "iPod sync is complete. OK to disconnect." in the Status pane at the top of the screen.

⊙ *To learn more about syncing iTunes and your device,* **see** *"Syncing Your iPod, iPhone, or iPad with iTunes" (in Chapter 9).*

 TELL ME MORE Media 1.5—Can I Use iTunes with a Non-iPod MP3 Player?

Access this audio recording through your registered Web Edition at **my.safaribooksonline.com/9780132660273/media**.

Figure 1.11   *The Summary page for an iPhone during a sync*

iTunes isn't much fun without content—music to listen to and videos to watch. Learn how to fill up your iTunes library with all your favorite albums, movies, and more.

2

Getting Content into iTunes

A music and video player is only as good as the content you play on it. To get the most out of iTunes, you'll want to fill it with your favorite music, movies, TV shows, and more. And that's what this chapter is all about.

For many people, iTunes means music, so you'll learn different ways to get your tunes into iTunes: from a CD, the Internet, or folders where it's already stored on your computer. You'll also learn how to optimize import settings so your music sounds its best.

An album collection is kind of boring without the eye-popping artwork on the covers. This chapter tells you how to get cover artwork into iTunes and match it with the correct album. (You can even add extra pictures, such as photos from a concert, if you want.)

Moving beyond music, the chapter ends with how to add other kinds of content: movies, TV shows, and podcasts. By the time you're done, you'll have a full library. Now if only iTunes could help you find time to listen to and watch it all!

Importing Music from a CD

If you've spent years building an impressive CD collection of all your favorite music, you probably won't want to start from scratch with iTunes. Luckily, it's easy to import music from your CDs into iTunes.

Getting songs from your CDs into iTunes is called *ripping*—but really, it's more of a snap. Fire up iTunes and insert an audio CD into your computer's CD/DVD drive. A track list automatically appears in the main iTunes window, and if you're connected to the Internet, iTunes also fills in song titles and information about each track, including the artist, album, and genre. At the same time, a dialog box appears, asking whether you want to import the CD to your iTunes library (see Figure 2.1). Click Yes, and iTunes copies the songs from your CD to iTunes.

The process may take a few minutes; you can do other things on your computer—check your email, surf the web, work on a business plan or your Great American

Novel, or even listen to other music in iTunes—while iTunes rips the CD tracks in the background. You can see how many songs iTunes has imported by looking to the left of the song titles. A white checkmark inside a green circle means that the song has made it into iTunes. iTunes also shows you how the import is progressing in the Status pane at the top of the screen. After iTunes has imported all the tracks, it plays a tone to let you know it's done. Now you can remove the CD from the CD-ROM drive.

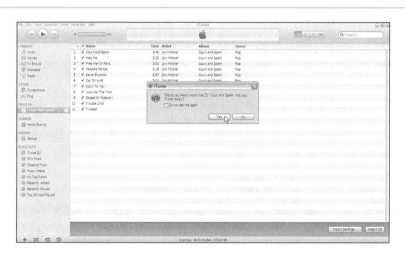

Figure 2.1   *When you insert a CD, iTunes displays a track list and asks if you want to import the album.*

☉ *You can tell iTunes to eject a CD automatically when it's done ripping tracks,* **see** *"Fine-Tuning CD Import Settings," coming up in this chapter.*

If the dialog box doesn't appear when you insert a music CD into your computer (or if you accidentally close the box or click No), you can start an import by clicking the lower-right Import CD button.

  SHOW ME   Media 2.1—Importing Music into iTunes from a CD
Access this video file through your registered Web Edition at
my.safaribooksonline.com/9780132660273/media.

 **LET ME TRY IT**

Selecting Songs to Import

Love some songs on an album but hate others? Here's how you can pick and choose, importing only the songs you want into your iTunes library:

1. Insert a CD into your computer's CD/DVD drive.

2. When the iTunes dialog box asks whether you want to import the CD, click No.

3. In the track list, click the checkmark to the left of any tracks you *don't* want. iTunes won't import unchecked tracks.

4. Click the lower-right Import CD button.

That's all it takes—iTunes imports only those tracks that have a checkmark and skips any unchecked ones.

> Want to import just one track from a whole CD? Here's a shortcut so you won't waste time unchecking tracks one by one. Press the Ctrl key (Cmd on a Mac) and hold it down as you click any checkmark—*all* the checkmarks disappear. Now click the check box of the song you want to select it, and click Import CD.

Fine-Tuning CD Import Settings

For most people, the iTunes default settings for importing music from CDs work just fine. But you can tweak CD import settings to suit your preferences. Maybe you want iTunes to eject a CD automatically after ripping its tracks, for example. Or you might want the highest-quality sound, even if it takes up a ton of space, for songs you plan to burn to an audio CD, such as a custom playlist you're creating for your own use. You can adjust the settings in general or change them before you import a particular CD that you want to handle differently than usual.

 LET ME TRY IT

Adjusting Your CD Import Settings

Here's how to change the iTunes settings for importing audio CDs:

1. In iTunes, select Edit, Preferences, General (on a PC), or iTunes, Preferences, General (on a Mac). This opens the dialog box shown in Figure 2.2.

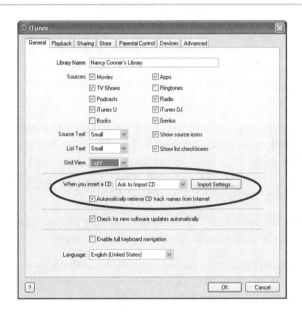

Figure 2.2   *Here's where you set your preferences for importing CD tracks.*

2. Make a selection from the When You Insert a CD drop-down list. This selec-
    tion tells iTunes how to behave when you put a new CD into your com-
    puter's CD/DVD drive. Here are your options:

    Show CD—iTunes shows that you've inserted the CD and lists its tracks,
    but doesn't do anything with the disc. If you tend to edit track information
    before you import a CD, choose this setting.

    ⓖ *See "Tagging Tracks with Optional Tags" (in Chapter 7, "Organizing Your Content")
    to find out how to edit track information in iTunes.*

    Begin Playing—This setting tells iTunes to start playing any CD as soon as
    you insert it. This setting won't import any tracks from the CD.

    ⓖ *For more about playing CDs through iTunes,* ***see*** *"Listening to a CD" (in Chapter 4,
    "Listening in iTunes").*

    Ask to Import CD—This is the default behavior; when you put a CD into
    your computer, iTunes shows a dialog box asking whether you want to
    import the CD into iTunes.

    Import CD—If you're happy with the iTunes import settings (as you
    should be by the time you've made your way through the steps in this list),

you might want to choose this setting. As soon as you insert a CD into your computer, iTunes starts importing it (without asking permission first).

Import CD and Eject—This option comes in handy when you're moving a big batch of CDs into iTunes. When you insert a CD, iTunes imports it automatically. When it finishes the import, it spits out the CD, ready for the next one.

3. Make sure there's a check in the check box labeled Automatically Retrieve CD Track Names from the Internet. This action saves you tons of time when you're importing CDs—you don't have to go through and type in song titles, artist names, and so on by hand, because iTunes gets them for you automatically. This box is checked by default.

4a. If you just wanted to tell iTunes how to react when you insert a CD, you're done. Click OK and skip the rest of the steps in this list.

4b. If you want to adjust how iTunes handles the actual files it imports, you have a few more steps to go. Click the Import Settings button to open the Import Settings dialog box, shown in Figure 2.3.

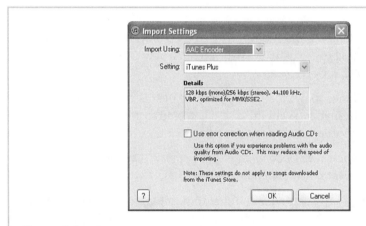

Figure 2.3 *The Import Settings dialog box*

5. Make a selection from the Import Using drop-down list:

AAC Encoder—For listening via iTunes on your computer or on your iPod, this is a great choice. AAC stands for *Advanced Audio Coding*, and it provides more compression (so files are smaller) and better sound quality than MP3. AAC is the iTunes default format. When you use the AAC encoder to import audio, choose High Quality or iTunes Plus (the default) from the Setting drop-down list. Both of these settings produce decent sound; iTunes Plus produces somewhat bigger files.

AIFF Encoder—Choose AIFF (Audio Interchange File Format) if you're going to use a Mac to transfer your audio files to a CD or DVD; it's a proprietary format developed by Apple. AIFF provides the highest sound quality but produces huge files (taking up about 10MB per minute), so it's not a good choice for importing songs that you'll listen to on your iPod, iPhone, or iPad. In fact, some iPods, such as the first- and second-generation iPod Shuffle, won't play this format. If you do use AIFF to encode songs you're importing, you'll get the best results if you select Automatic from the Setting drop-down list.

Apple Lossless Encoder—This is a good format for songs you're going to put on a CD or play on your iPod, iPhone, or iPad. Apple Lossless files are smaller than AIFF files yet retain the fidelity of the original file. If you choose this format, your only choice in the Setting drop-down list is Automatic.

MP3 Encoder—All MP3 players support MP3 format, so this is a good, versatile choice. For the best playback, choose High Quality or Higher Quality from the Setting drop-down list (the higher the quality, though, the bigger the file).

Compressed audio files are either lossy or lossless. *Lossy* means that, during compression, the file size is reduced by permanently discarding bits of information considered redundant or unnecessary. *Lossless,* as the name implies, keeps all data from the original file in the compressed file. Lossy files are smaller, but because some data is discarded, the quality is slightly less than the original—although most listeners are unlikely to detect any difference. Lossless files reproduce the original file, including every bit of data, when the file is uncompressed. AAC and MP3 files are lossy; the other formats in this list are lossless.

WAV Encoder—The WAV format is the Windows equivalent of AIFF; it produces high-quality sound at the cost of lots of space. It's a good choice if you're going to use a PC to burn songs to an audio CD and you want the highest quality. When you choose this format, select Automatic from the Import Using drop-down list.

6. Choose the settings you want from the Setting drop-down list. The items on this list change according to what you selected in Import Using. Make your choice based on the previous recommendations.

7. If you want automatic error correction, put a check mark in the check box labeled Use Error Correction When Reading Audio CDs. Turning on this setting can help improve the quality of your audio and minimize skipping.

8. When everything looks good, click OK to apply your import settings. Click OK again to apply your general preferences.

iTunes applies your settings and uses them the next time you import tracks from an audio CD. If you've changed the import settings for a single transfer, don't forget to change them back to your standard settings when you're done.

Making an Album Gapless

If you're listening to a live recording of a concert, you want to hear the event as it happened, without any pauses or fade-outs between songs. When you make an album *gapless,* the songs move smoothly from one right to the next, without pausing.

 SHOW ME   Media 2.2—Making an Album Gapless
Access this video file through your registered Web Edition at
my.safaribooksonline.com/9780132660273/media.

 LET ME TRY IT

Removing Gaps from an Album

When you want an album to be gapless, you need to tell iTunes before it starts the import. If you've turned off the dialog box that appears when you insert a CD (the one that asks whether you want to import the CD), turn it back on: Select Edit, Preferences (on a PC) or iTunes, Preferences (on a Mac); make sure the General tab is selected, and select Ask to Import CD from the When You Insert a CD drop-down list. When that's all set, follow these steps:

1. Insert the CD you want to import.

2. When the dialog box asking whether you want to import the CD appears, click No. (You don't want to import it yet because you must set up your import as gapless first.)

3. Make sure the CD is selected in the left-hand iTunes source list and select File, Get Info (or press Ctrl+I or Cmd-I).

4. In the CD Info dialog box, shown in Figure 2.4, select the Gapless Album
    check box.

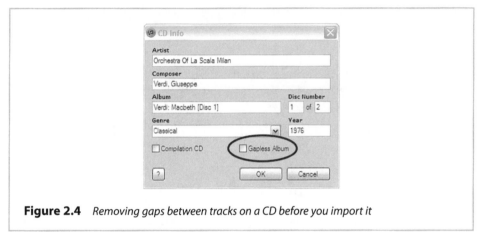

Figure 2.4   *Removing gaps between tracks on a CD before you import it*

5. Click OK.

6. Click Import CD (in the bottom-right corner of the iTunes screen).

iTunes imports the tracks on the CD. When you play them in iTunes or on your iPod,
the playback moves seamlessly from one track to the next.

 LET ME TRY IT

Making Selected Tracks Gapless

If you want to make only some of a CD's tracks gapless when you import them,
here's what to do:

1. Insert the CD you want to import.

2. When the dialog box asking whether you want to import the CD appears,
    click No. (If you don't see this dialog box and the import starts automati-
    cally, click the lower-right Stop Import button.)

3. In the album's track list, select the songs you want to make gapless. (To
    select contiguous songs, select the first song in the group and hold down
    the Shift key as you select the last song in the group. To select multiple
    songs, hold down the Ctrl key on a PC or the Cmd key on a Mac as you
    select the songs you want.)

4. Select File, Get Info.

5. If a warning about editing multiple items appears, click Yes.

6. In the Multiple Item Information dialog box, click the Options tab, shown in Figure 2.5.

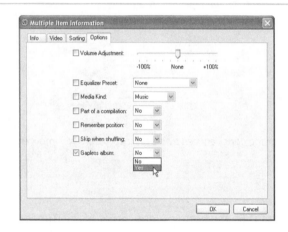

Figure 2.5 *Making selected songs gapless*

7. From the Gapless Album drop-down list, select Yes.

8. Click OK.

9. Back in the main iTunes screen, click Import CD.

If you want to remove gaps by combining several tracks into a single file, try this: Before you rip the CD, make sure that the tracks are sorted by track number (in the CD's track list, click the header of the leftmost column). Choose the tracks you want to combine (using the Shift or Ctrl/Cmd key as you click them). Then select Advanced, Join CD Tracks. Click Import CD. iTunes rips the multiple tracks and imports them as one file.

Importing Music That's Stored on Your Computer

Importing songs from a CD isn't the only way to get your music into iTunes. If you have songs already stored on your computer—music you downloaded from a band's website or an online retailer such as Amazon.com, for example—you can move those tunes into your iTunes library.

iTunes offers a couple different ways to get music from other places on your computer into iTunes:

- Using the iTunes File menu
- Dragging and dropping

The following sections cover your options.

 SHOW ME   Media 2.3—Transferring Files from Your Computer into iTunes
Access this video file through your registered Web Edition at
my.safaribooksonline.com/9780132660273/media.

Importing Music Using the File Menu

One way to get your computer's music into iTunes is to start with the File menu.

 LET ME TRY IT

Moving Songs from a Folder on Your Computer into iTunes

You can navigate to the songs you want and move them into iTunes with just a few clicks:

1. In iTunes, select File, Add File to Library.

2. In the Add to Library dialog box, shown in Figure 2.6, find the track you want to add. (To choose multiple tracks, hold down the Shift or Ctrl/Cmd key as you make your selections.)

3. Click Open.

iTunes copies the files you selected and organizes them for you in your iTunes library. The original file is still in the folder where you found it.

If the file you're transferring is in a format that iTunes can't play, such as Windows Media Audio (WMA) format, iTunes asks whether you want to convert the file you're importing. Click Convert if you want an iTunes-playable version in your iTunes library. Clicking Convert doesn't affect the original file—just the version you import into iTunes.

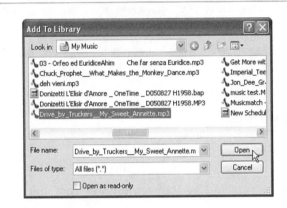

Figure 2.6   *In the Add to Library dialog box (shown here in Windows), select the tracks you want to import.*

Dragging Files into iTunes

When you want to import a song, using the drag-and-drop method is even quicker and easier than starting with the File menu. Just find the tunes you want and drag them over to iTunes.

 LET ME TRY IT

Dragging Songs into iTunes on a Mac

Here's how to drag music files into iTunes on a Mac:

1. Use the Finder to select the files you want (individual songs, groups of songs, folders, or volumes).

2. Drag your selections to the iTunes icon in your Dock and drop them there.

iTunes opens and brings your files into its library. If you already have iTunes open, just drag your selection into the main window to get it into iTunes.

LET ME TRY IT

Dragging Songs into iTunes on a PC

If you're a Windows user, follow these steps to drag your tunes into iTunes:

1. Start up iTunes and open Windows Explorer.

2. In Windows Explorer, find the files you want to import into iTunes. You can select a single song, a range of songs, or an entire folder.

3. Drag your selections into the iTunes window and drop them there.

If you've pinned the iTunes icon to your Windows Start menu, you can simply drag your selection to the icon and drop it on top. When you do this, iTunes starts up and imports the files to its library.

Importing Content from the Internet

Say you're cruising around the Internet and you visit the website of a new local band. They're offering free downloads of their latest song, and you want to get that song into iTunes.

Easy. Download the song to your computer, making note of where you stored it. Then follow the steps listed in the previous section, "Importing Music That's Stored on Your Computer," to put your new song in your iTunes library. Use this technique for any audio or video file you want to store in iTunes—albums, podcasts, video clips, whatever. If you can download it to your computer, you can store it in iTunes.

🄶 *Of course, you can also purchase music in the iTunes Store—**see** Chapter 3, "Shopping in the iTunes Store," to learn all about that.*

Importing Playlists from Another Program

If you've switched to iTunes from a different media player and organizer, you've probably compiled some playlists in your old program that you'd like to transfer to iTunes. If the program that holds your playlists can export them in M3U format (most can), you can move your playlists into iTunes.

M3U is a computer file format that stores playlists whose individual files end with the .mp3 file extension. Many programs support the M3U format.

LET ME TRY IT

Importing a Playlist into iTunes

Before you can import a playlist from another media program into iTunes, you need to make sure that the playlist's tracks are already in your iTunes Library.

💬 *To find out how to import files into iTunes,* **see** *"Importing Music That's Stored on Your Computer," earlier in this chapter.*

When the files are in place, follow these steps:

1. Open your non-iTunes media program and export the playlists you want from that program, making sure the playlists you're exporting are in M3U format. The specific steps for exporting a playlist depend on your program. Note where you save the playlist file on your computer.

2. In iTunes, select File, Library, Import Playlist.

3. In the Import dialog box, browse to find your playlist file. Select it and click Open.

iTunes imports your playlist. Your new iTunes playlist has the same name as the M3U file.

💬 *Read all about playlists in Chapter 5, "Playing with Playlists."*

Finding Music You've Imported

Okay, you've moved some music into iTunes. Where is it now? iTunes stores your imported music tracks in the iTunes Music folder. Where's that?

*   **Mac users**—On a Mac, your music is stored inside your Mac OS X User folder. Here's the file path: *yourname*/Music/iTunes/iTunes Music.

*   **Windows 7 and Vista users**—In Windows 7 or Vista, you'll find your songs in your Music folder: *yourname*/Music/iTunes/iTunes Media.

*   **Windows XP users**—In Windows XP, look in your My Music folder, following this file path: *yourname*/My Music/iTunes/iTunes Media/Music.

In all cases, replace *yourname* with the actual username you use on your computer.

> You can always find the location of your iTunes Media folder from within iTunes. Select Edit, Preferences (in Windows) or iTunes, Preferences (on a Mac) and click Advanced. The iTunes Media Folder location box shows the full address for the folder.

Adding Cover Art

Part of the pleasure of collecting albums is collecting the art that graces their covers. Album cover art can be funky, fun, beautiful, or just plain weird. Storing your music on your computer (or your iPod, iPhone, or iPad) doesn't mean you can't enjoy the albums' cover art. iTunes can display covers as well as play songs.

When you're connected to the Internet as you rip CDs, or when you buy music and other content through the iTunes Store, iTunes automatically adds the cover art to the album.

You can also tell iTunes to fetch the art for a particular album. (Maybe you weren't connected to the Internet when you imported the CD or iTunes failed to download the cover for some reason.) First, make sure that you're signed in to your Apple account. Then, in your iTunes Library, select the item whose cover art you want. Click Advanced, Get Album Artwork, or right-click (Ctrl-click) the item and select Get Album Artwork from the context menu.

ⓒ *If you don't yet have an Apple ID,* **see** *"Creating Your iTunes Store Account" (in Chapter 3) to set one up.*

The first time you tell iTunes to fetch an album's artwork, a dialog box appears and asks whether you're sure you want to do this. The reason for this caution is that Apple wants you to know that you're sending information about the item over the Internet to Apple, which needs this info to retrieve the artwork. Apple doesn't store information about the album, though.

If you don't want to see the dialog box appear every time you request album artwork, select the Do Not Ask Me Again box and then click Get Album Artwork to proceed.

Adding Artwork Automatically

You can tell iTunes to automatically grab the cover art for items you import to your iTunes Library so you don't have spend time doing it manually.

 **LET ME TRY IT**

Getting Album Art Automatically

To have iTunes automatically find and add album art to music ripped from CDs and added to your library, follow these steps:

1. In iTunes, select Edit, Preferences on a PC, or iTunes, Preferences on a Mac.

2. Click the Store tab, shown in Figure 2.7.

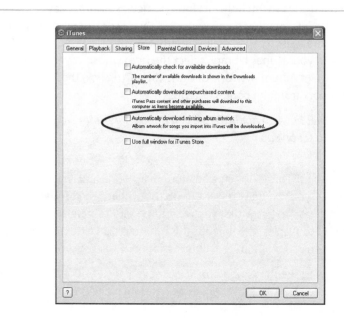

Figure 2.7   *Telling iTunes to automatically retrieve the cover artwork for CDs you import into your library*

3. Select the Automatically Download Missing Artwork check box.

4. A dialog box appears, making sure you're okay with sending Apple info about which songs are missing artwork. Click Enable Automatic Down-loading.

5. Click OK.

From now on, when you import a CD (and you're online and signed in to your Apple account), iTunes grabs the cover artwork and adds it to the album in your library.

Manually Adding Album Art

If you're an eclectic collector of rare music, you may find that iTunes can't retrieve the cover art for some of your albums. That doesn't mean that you're doomed to flip through one "unknown album" after another, trying to find the one you want (not much fun in Cover Flow view). If you can get an image of the cover, you can match the artwork with its album.

First, get an image of the cover artwork. You can scan this in from your physical music collection (size it to 300x300 pixels). You can also look around the Internet for stock cover art, on sites such as Google Images (http://images.google.com), artist/band sites, or retail sites that sell music.

When you've found the cover artwork, go to your iTunes Library and make sure your Artwork Viewer is open. (If you don't see this pane in the lower-left corner, click the up arrow on the left side of the status bar to display it.) Select the item (or items) you want to add the artwork to, and take one of these actions:

- **Drag and drop**—Drag the image from its location to the Artwork Viewer and drop it there.

- **Add artwork to a single item**—If you're adding artwork to just one track, select File, Get Info. In the dialog box that opens, click the Artwork tab, shown in Figure 2.8. You can drag the image into the box on this tab and drop it there. Or click Add, browse your folders to find the image you want, and click Open. The image appears in the box. Click OK to add it to the item.

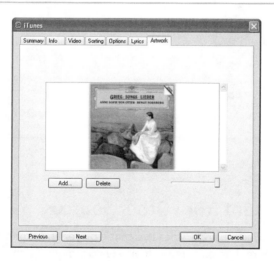

Figure 2.8   *Add or delete artwork for a single item on the Artwork tab*

If you want to remove existing artwork that's associated with an item in your iTunes Library, you can do that from the Artwork tab as well. When you choose File, Get Info and click Artwork, the tab displays current artwork for the selected item. Click the image to select it, click Delete, and then click OK. iTunes removes the image from the item.

- **Add multiple pieces of art to an item**—You can add more than one piece of art to an item in your library. Maybe you want to include the back cover or some photos from the album notes, for example. When you want to add more artwork to an item, select the item you want and click File, Get Info. Then proceed as described in the previous point.

- **Add the same artwork to multiple items**—Hold down the Ctrl key (on a PC) or the Command key (on a Mac) to select the items you want. Select File, Get Info. The first time you do this, a dialog box appears, making sure you want to edit the info for multiple items at once. Click Yes. The Multiple Item Information dialog box, shown in Figure 2.9, opens. Find the artwork you want and drag it into the Artwork box on the right. Click OK to add the art to all the items you selected.

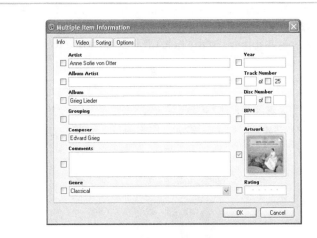

Figure 2.9   *Adding artwork to multiple items*

Getting Content from Other Sources

You may be happy just using iTunes as a music player and organizer. But iTunes does so much more than play music. It also plays movies, TV shows, music videos, podcasts, and more—if you can watch it or listen to it, you can probably use it in iTunes. This section shows you how to get these kinds of content into iTunes.

Ripping DVDs

iTunes makes ripping CDs so easy, you might be surprised to learn that there's no way to rip a DVD in iTunes. That's thanks, at least in part, to U.S. law: The Digital Millennium Copyright Act makes it illegal to circumvent a DVD whose contents are protected by a copy protection scheme. In other words, if the DVD manufacturer takes steps to prevent users from copying the DVD's content, you're not supposed to get around that protection.

Even though Fair Use allows you to make a backup copy of a DVD that you own (as long as it's for your own, personal use and you don't distribute it to anyone else), you can't rip the contents from a protected DVD. Most commercial DVDs are protected by CSS (content scramble system) encryption, so that means you can't legally copy their contents if you live in the U.S.

Other countries' copyright laws vary. Before you rip a DVD, make sure you know what's legal where you live.

Although iTunes won't rip DVDs, other available programs will. If you're sure you're not violating any copyright laws, you can use one of these programs to copy a DVD's contents, store the copy on your computer, and then transfer the stored copy to your iTunes library. Table 2.1 shows some popular DVD-ripping programs.

Table 2.1 DVD-Ripping Programs

Program	Supports Windows	Supports Mac	Cost	Website
AnyDVD	98, Me, XP, Vista, Windows 7	No	€49 for a 2-year subscription	www.slysoft.com
CloneDVD	98, Me, XP, Vista, Windows 7	No	€49 for a 2-year subscription	www.slysoft.com
Clone2Go DVD Ripper	NT, 2000, XP, 2003, Vista, Windows 7	OS X 10.5 or higher	$39.95	www.clone2go.com
Daniusoft DVD Ripper	2000, 2003, XP, Vista, Windows 7	OS X 10.4 or higher	$39.95	www.daniusoft.com
DVD Copy	2000, XP, Vista, Windows 7	No	$50	www.dvdfab.com
RipIt	No	OS X 10.5 or higher	$19.95	http://thelittleappfactory.com
Wondershare DVD Ripper Platinum	NT4, 2000, 2003, XP, Vista, Windows 7	No	$39.95	www.wondershare.com
Wondershare DVD Ripper for Mac	No	OS X 10.5 or higher	$45	www.wondershare.com

Don't break the law to get a copy of your favorite movie into iTunes. If you're not sure that copying a DVD counts as fair use, purchase a copy that you can download to your computer. The iTunes Store has thousands of movies for sale or rent, as Chapter 3 explains.

Importing a Digital Copy from a DVD

Some movie companies include a second disc when you buy a DVD. This disc is a digital copy, and you can legally copy its contents to iTunes without messing with the DVD's copy protections. Usually, a DVD box tells you right on the cover whether it contains a digital copy.

You can use the digital copy disc to save a copy of the video in iTunes. Before you can save a digital copy of a movie to your iTunes library using this method, you need to be signed in to your iTunes Store account.

 Need to set up an account at the iTunes Store? **See** "Creating Your iTunes Store Account" (in Chapter 3).

 LET ME TRY IT

Importing a Digital Copy of a Movie or TV Show

When you buy a DVD with a digital copy, here's how to transfer the digital copy to iTunes:

1. Sign in to your iTunes Store account.

2. Insert the digital copy disc into your computer's CD/DVD drive.

3. Select the digital copy disc in the iTunes Source list that appears. This opens a screen that lets you import the video.

4. In the Enter Code box, type in the code that came with your disc. Then click Redeem.

iTunes imports the video into iTunes. You can find it in the appropriate section of your iTunes library (Movies or TV Shows). Now you can watch it, free and clear of any legal hassles.

 Read about how to watch movies and TV shows in iTunes in Chapter 6, "Viewing in iTunes: TV, Movies, and More."

Importing a Podcast from the Internet

A *podcast* is a periodic audio or video broadcast over the Internet. If you listen to a favorite podcast on your computer, you can easily subscribe to that podcast through iTunes. One way to subscribe is through the iTunes Store, but if you know the website where the podcast is based, you can direct iTunes to subscribe right from the source.

Ⓖ *To read about how to find podcasts and subscribe to them through your iTunes Store account,* **see** *"Subscribing to Podcasts" (Chapter 3).*

 LET ME TRY IT

Subscribing to a Podcast Through iTunes

Here's how to subscribe to a podcast using iTunes (no iTunes Store account needed):

1. In iTunes, select Advanced, Subscribe to Podcast to open the Subscribe to Podcast dialog box.

2. Go to the website that hosts the podcast you want. Copy its address from your web browser's address bar. (Select the web address and press Ctrl+C on a PC or Cmd-C on a Mac.)

3. Back in the Subscribe to Podcast dialog box, paste the podcast's web address into the URL box. (Click inside the box and press Ctrl+C on a PC or Cmd-C on a Mac.)

4. Click OK.

Ⓖ *To learn how to adjust the settings for podcasts you subscribe to,* **see** *"Choosing Podcast Settings" (in Chapter 4).*

The iTunes Store offers one-stop shopping for all your entertainment needs. Buy music, videos, and more—from the latest hits to the classics—to enjoy on your computer or your iPod.

3

Shopping in the iTunes Store

After you've transferred your entire existing media library to iTunes, what next? You'll probably want to get the latest releases and maybe find old favorites you don't yet own. No need to drive to the mall to do that. The iTunes Store lets you buy music and videos, and download them directly to your computer or iTunes Store–compatible portable device (that means the iPod Touch, iPhone, or iPad).

This chapter introduces you to the iTunes Store—what you can buy there, how to set up an account, and how the store is organized. Then you'll learn how to browse and search for items, preview them, and (if you want) buy them. Parents will be glad to learn that they can set up a monthly iTunes allowance for their kids and implement parental controls so their children aren't downloading inappropriate content. You'll also get the scoop on how to set up a Wish List, buy or redeem iTunes gifts, and buy content directly from your iPod Touch, iPhone, or iPad.

Ready to go shopping? Read on.

What Can You Buy?

Lots of people think iTunes is all about music (no surprise there, given its name). And although music is probably the highest-volume, most dynamic part of the iTunes Store, you may be surprised by the variety of material you can buy there. Check out the possibilities:

- **Music**—Whether you want songs, serenades, or symphonies, the iTunes Store probably has what you're looking for, with songs and albums in nearly two dozen musical genres, from alternative to jazz, to hiphop, to world music. You'll find songs and music videos in this part of the store.

- **Movies**—Look in the Movies section of the iTunes Store to find your favorite flicks, from the classics to the latest releases. You can buy a movie or rent it. The iTunes Store has high-definition movies, too, for the clearest, sharpest picture.

- **TV Shows**—Buy past seasons or individual shows. As with movies, you can rent some TV shows.

- **Apps**—If you've ever thought "I wish I could . . . " about your iPhone or iPad, there's probably already an app for that. Find games, productivity apps, utilities, social networking tools, and a whole lot more.

- **Podcasts**—If you like to listen to podcasts, you'll find tons of audio and video podcasts to choose from in the iTunes Store, and most are free. You can listen to individual podcasts or subscribe to a series.

- **Audiobooks**—If you like to listen to your books, you'll be happy to see iTunes Store's great selection of audiobooks. Download a book to your iPod, iPhone, or iPad, and listen to it on the go.

- **Educational content**—The iTunes U section of the iTunes Store is all about learning: You can listen to lectures from top professors, practice a language, and hear podcasts from museums and other cultural institutions—all without spending a dime.

 TELL ME MORE   Media 3.1—How You Can Use Your iTunes Purchases
Access this audio recording through your registered Web Edition at
my.safaribooksonline.com/9780132660273/media.

Creating Your iTunes Store Account

Before you can begin shopping in the iTunes Store, you need to set up an account. Your iTunes Store account provides you with an Apple ID that you can use to make purchases not just in the iTunes Store, but the App Store and the online Apple Store as well.

 LET ME TRY IT

Setting Up an iTunes Store Account

To create your iTunes Store account, follow these steps:

1. Open iTunes and, in the left source list, click iTunes Store to open the iTunes Store home page, shown in Figure 3.1.

2. Click the upper-right Sign In command.

3. In the iTunes dialog box (see Figure 3.2), click Create New Account.

Figure 3.1   *The iTunes Store home page*

If you already have an Apple ID (maybe you've created an account with the Apps Store or another Apple service), you can use that ID for your iTunes Store account. When you see the iTunes dialog box, type in your Apple ID and password, and click Sign In. Apple uses the information from your existing account to sign you in to the iTunes Store.

Figure 3.2   *Sign in with your Apple ID and password, or create a new account.*

4. iTunes opens a page welcoming you to the iTunes Store. Click Continue.

5. Read the iTunes Store's terms, conditions, and privacy policy, and then select the box that says you've read them and agree to them. Click Continue.

> You can print the iTunes Store terms and policies and read them at your leisure. Click the left Printable Version link to open the document in a web browser. You can print a hard copy from there.

6. On the Create Apple ID page, fill in the personal info Apple needs to set up your account. This includes your email address; a password (this has to be at least eight characters and include at least one letter, one number, and one capital letter); a security question of your choice (along with the right answer), in case you forget your password later; and your birth date. You can also opt into or out of email lists for Apple and the iTunes Store. When everything looks good, click Continue.

7. Enter your credit card information so you can pay for your iTunes Store purchases. Click Continue.

After you've created your account, iTunes takes you back to the iTunes Store home page (see Figure 3.1). It's time to go shopping!

> You can change the language in which the iTunes Store displays its content. To pick a different language, scroll down to the bottom of any page in the iTunes Store. In the far-right corner is a button that indicates the current language. The button is in the form of a flag. If you're in the United States, for example, the button shows an American flag to indicate U.S. English. Click the flag button to open a page showing all the languages iTunes supports. Click any language to make that language the new default in your iTunes Store.

Finding Your Way Around

Just like any large brick-and-mortar store, the iTunes Store is divided into departments, each featuring a particular kind of content: Music, Movies, TV Shows, App Store, Podcasts, Audiobooks, and iTunes U. These departments are listed in a horizontal bar that stretches across the top of every page in the store. To go to a section of the Store, click its name in the bar; the iTunes Store opens the home page for that section.

To get back to the main iTunes page, click the far-left Home icon, a little picture of a house.

On the right side of the page is a sidebar that changes according to which section of the iTunes Store you're in. Here you'll find convenient Quick Links to help you zero in on the content you're looking for, as well as top sellers in various categories.

The middle of each section's home page shows featured items in different subcategories. Here you'll find new releases, sales, popular items, and (after you've made a few purchases) recommendations based on what you've bought.

Shopping for Music...and More

Remember the old days when you had to trudge to a record store or video rental shop to get your entertainment fix? Those days are long gone, now that iTunes brings a world of entertainment choices to you at home—or even when you're on the road. Digital downloads mean that you can get your music or movies within minutes and start enjoying them right away.

 SHOW ME   Media 3.2—Finding Items in the iTunes Store
Access this video file through your registered Web Edition at
my.safaribooksonline.com/9780132660273/media.

Browsing for Music

To check out featured selections in a particular music category, go to the black bar at the top of the iTunes Store screen. Point at Music, and a down arrow appears; click the arrow. You'll see a menu of categories—such as Alternative, Blues, Classical, Country, HipHop/Rap, Rock, and so on—as shown in Figure 3.3. Click the category you want to browse to open its page.

That's the quickest way to browse and see what's new. If you're looking for something more specific, such as a particular subgenre or the work of a specific artist, start on the iTunes Store home page; go to the far-right Quick Links section and click Browse. This opens a page like the one shown in Figure 3.4.

Because you're browsing for music, click Music in the left iTunes Store column. When you do that, other columns relevant to music appear: Genre, Subgenre, Artist, and Album. Narrow your options by selecting an item from each column. As you make your selections, the iTunes Store populates the next column with relevant choices. When you select an album, its songs appear in the lower pane.

Figure 3.3   *Select a category to browse*

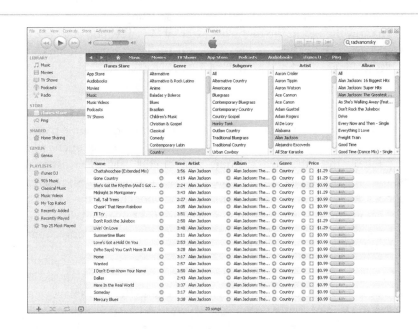

Figure 3.4   *Browsing music by genre, subgenre, artist, and album*

Want to preview a track? Double-click it to hear a 30-second sample.

◉ *If you're ready to buy,* **see** *"Buying Music and Other Media," coming up in this chapter.*

Searching for Music and Other Content

On some shopping excursions, you just want to browse. Other times, though, you want to do a highly targeted find-and-purchase mission: Get in, buy your music, and get out. When you know exactly what you want, this section tells you how to find it.

Doing a Quick Search

Imagine that you want to buy the song you slow-danced to at your high school prom. You remember the name of the tune (or part of it), but you're not sure about the artist or the album. When you know exactly what you're looking for in the iTunes Store, the upper-right Search Store box can help you find it. Type in all or part of a song title or artist name, and press Enter. iTunes searches its store and opens a page displaying the results.

The results page, shown in Figure 3.5, shows items from throughout the iTunes Store—not just songs, but albums, audiobooks, ebooks (if you've downloaded iBooks), music videos, movies, TV episodes, and anything else related to your search term. To narrow the results, go to the left Filter by Media section and click the category you want (such as Music, to find that long-ago prom song). Doing so narrows the results to show only the ones in the category you picked.

Using Power Search

To get focused results, do a Power Search. On the iTunes Store home page, go to the Quick Links section on the right and click Power Search. This opens a Power Search page like the one shown in Figure 3.6. From the drop-down list on the left, choose the type of product you're looking for: Music, Movies, TV Shows, Apps, Audiobooks, Podcasts, or iTunes U. Depending on your choice, the search boxes change so you can type in information specific to that category. When you select Music, for example, you can search by Artist, Composer, Song, Album, Genre, or any combination of these. Click Search to see the results.

Power Searches work for all kinds of iTunes Store content, not just music. When you choose a Power Search for a particular kind of content, iTunes displays categories relevant to the kind of content you chose. If you do a Power Search for movies, for example, you can search by Movie Title, Actor, Director/Producer, Description, Genre, and/or Rating. If you're looking for a podcast, you can search by Title, Author (podcaster), Description, Category (Arts, Business, News & Politics, and so on), Language, and so on.

Figure 3.5 *A quick search, using the upper-right Search Store box, shows results from across the iTunes Store.*

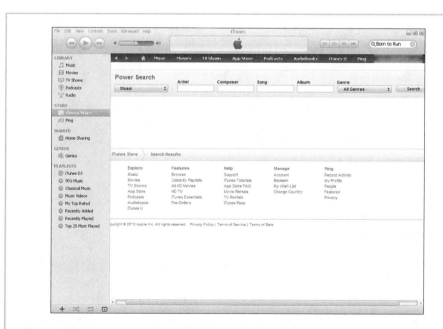

Figure 3.6 *Power Search options for Music*

Other Ways to Discover Music

On the home page of the iTunes Store Music section, the Quick Links section on the right offers a range of ways to find the music you want:

- **Just Added**—Click this link to see new releases added to iTunes during the last four weeks, shown in four separate columns. Click the Filter By dropdown list to see new releases for a specific genre.

- **Bargain songs and albums**—If you're craving some new tunes but don't have a ton of money to spend, take a look at what's on sale (or available for free) on iTunes right now. You'll find a mix of genres. Click one of these links to do some bargain hunting:

    - Free On iTunes

    - Albums Under $8

    - 69 Songs At 69¢

- **Celebrity Playlist Podcasts**—Ever wonder what songs Alicia Keys, Ringo Starr, Snoop Dogg, or Lady Gaga have on their iPods? Click this link to listen to free podcasts in which a range of celebrities discuss their favorite or most influential songs. You can also preview and purchase the songs mentioned in any podcast, as a playlist or just the tracks you liked.

> You can also browse celebrity playlists this way: On the iTunes Music home page, scroll down to the bottom of the page. Under Features, click Celebrity Playlists.

- **Ping Featured**—The new iTunes social networking site lets you find out what music your friends are buying. Clicking this link shows a list of featured artists and other members of the Ping community; you can follow them and see what they're up to.

To learn all about Ping, **see** Chapter 10, "Ping: iTunes Goes Social."

Protecting Your Kids

Parents, do you know what's on your kids' iPods? If you don't want them listening to music with explicit lyrics or watching R-rated movies or violent TV shows, you can set up iTunes so that it offers your kids only content you approve of.

And parental controls aren't just for kids. If graphic violence or sexual content makes you uncomfortable, you can tell the iTunes Store that you don't want to see any products with that kind of content.

SHOW ME   Media 3.3—Setting Parental Controls
Access this video file through your registered Web Edition at
my.safaribooksonline.com/9780132660273/media.

 LET ME TRY IT

Setting Parental Controls

To control the kind of content available on iTunes, follow these steps:

1. In Windows, select Edit, Preferences from the iTunes menu bar. On a Mac, select iTunes, Preferences. Or, if you like keyboard shortcuts, simply hold down the Ctrl key (on a PC) or the Command key (on a Mac) as you press the comma key.

2. Click the Parental Control tab, shown in Figure 3.7.

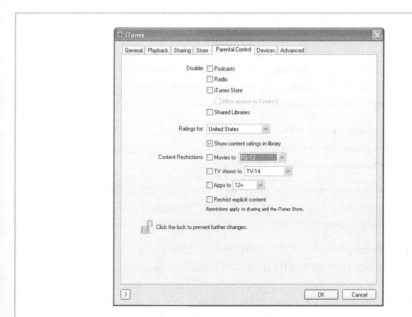

Figure 3.7   *Setting parental controls for iTunes and the iTunes Store*

3a. You can disable these iTunes options: podcasts, radio, the iTunes Store, and shared libraries. Click to put a check mark in the box beside any option that you want to disappear from iTunes.

3b. Optionally, you can choose the ratings given by a particular country. Select the country you want from the Ratings For drop-down list.

3c. If you want to keep the iTunes Store and/or sharing enabled but you want to restrict the content available, use the Content Restrictions section to set your preferences. Click to put check marks in the boxes next to the kind of content you want to restrict: movies, TV shows, apps, or explicit content.

4. To lock the preferences you've set, click the lock icon. That means no one but you (or whoever knows the administrator's password for your computer) can change these settings.

5. Type in the administrator's password for your computer.

6. Click OK to put your controls into effect.

Buying Music and Other Media

When you've found an item you're interested in, click the item to open its product page. (Figure 3.8 shows an example.) The product page has more information about a specific product. For an album, for example, the product page gives a description and lists tracks (along with information about each, such as artist, length, and popularity), and you can preview any or all tracks. For a movie, the product page lists the run time, file size, language, and rating; it may include a plot summary, credits, and any extras. Product pages also offer customer ratings and reviews, along with similar products you might like.

If you want to buy the product—whether it's an album, a movie, an audiobook, a podcast, or a TV series—click its Buy button. In Figure 3.8, you would click the Buy Album button just below the album's cover art.

If you're not currently signed in to your iTunes Store account, a dialog box appears, asking for your password. Type it in and click Get. (If you've previously told iTunes to remember your password, it's already filled in; just click the Get button.)

Next, you see a dialog box asking for confirmation that you want to buy the item (a welcome sight if you clicked Buy by mistake or thought you were downloading free content). Click OK to purchase your selection. iTunes charges your registered credit card and downloads your purchase, storing it in your iTunes Library and adding it to your Purchased playlist in the iTunes Store. Apple also sends you an email receipt for your purchase.

Ⓖ *To listen to files you've downloaded to your computer from the iTunes Store, whether they're music, a podcast, or an audiobook, **see** Chapter 4, "Listening in iTunes." To watch a movie or TV show, **see** Chapter 6, "Viewing in iTunes: TV, Movies, and More."*

Figure 3.8 *Setting parental controls for iTunes and the iTunes Store*

During the time it takes for your purchase to download to your computer, you can keep browsing the iTunes Store and buying other items. If you buy something else, iTunes adds it to the download queue.

Buying a Single Song or TV Episode

Music albums and some TV series let you buy a single song or episode instead of the whole package. To buy part of an album or series from its product page, look in the track list to find the individual item you want to purchase. In the far-right Price column is a Buy button that displays the item's price. Click Buy to purchase and download just that track.

> Some selections are available only if you buy the complete album or TV season. In these cases, instead of a Buy button, you'll see the words Album Only or Season Only.

Completing an Album

Say you've bought a favorite song, and then you decide you want to own the whole album. You've already bought one song, so of course, you don't want to pay for that song twice.

iTunes figures that you might want to try a song or two before you commit to an entire album, so they've made it easy to fill in what's missing—without paying double. On the home page of the iTunes Store Music section, go to Music Quick Links and click Complete My Album. This opens a page like the one shown in Figure 3.9, displaying albums from which you bought at least one song, along with the price for buying the rest of the songs on that album.

Click Complete My Album for the album you want to buy. This opens the album's page, with any songs you already own grayed out in the track list. Click Buy Album to proceed as you would when buying a whole album.

Figure 3.9   *The Complete My Album page*

Renting Movies and TV Shows

The good old days weren't always all that great. Remember waiting in line at the video store to rent the latest new release—if it was available? And then you had to rewind the tape and rush to return it before late fees kicked in. What a hassle, just to watch a movie or catch up on past seasons of a favorite TV series.

Those not-so-good old days are long gone. With iTunes, you can rent movies and TV shows from the comfort of home and watch them immediately. You even get your choice of how to watch them: on your computer; video iPod, iPhone, or iPad; or (if you're a subscriber) on Apple TV.

G *To learn more about Apple TV,* **see** *"Apple TV and iTunes" (in Chapter 6).*

If you just want to watch a movie or TV show, renting offers some distinct advantages over buying: It costs less (as little as 99 cents), and it doesn't clutter up your computer's hard disk with videos you'll never watch more than once.

Before you rent a video from the iTunes Store, keep these basics in mind:

- When you rent a movie or TV show, you have 30 days to watch it. After that time window, it disappears from your iTunes Library.

- After you've started watching a movie, you have 24 hours (in the U.S.) or 48 hours (in other countries) to finish it. If you don't watch the entire video within that time period, it's gone from your iTunes Library, and you'll have to rent it again if you want to see the rest.

- If you download a rental to your computer, you can transfer the video to another device, such as your iPod, iPhone, or iPad. (When you do, the movie disappears from your computer's iTunes Library. You can transfer it back again if you want, but it can exist on only one device at a time during the rental period.) If you download a rental directly to your iPhone 4, iPad, fourth-generation iPod Touch, or Apple TV, you must watch it on the device you downloaded it to—you can't transfer it to your computer or a different device.

- Want an encore performance? You can watch the movie as many times as you want during the allotted 24- or 48-hour window after you begin it.

The process of renting a movie or TV show is almost identical to the process of buying any kind of iTunes content. When you find a movie or TV show you want to watch, look for its Rent button (not all videos are available for rental). Click Rent and sign in to iTunes (if prompted), and iTunes starts the download. You can watch your movie or show right away.

Subscribing to Podcasts

A *podcast* is an audio or video program that gets released in episodes and that you can download and listen to or view on your computer or MP3 player. You can find as many kinds of podcasts as there are people with something to say: Topics include politics, arts, health, music, lifestyle, science, sports, religion and spirituality—and just about anything else you can imagine. The iTunes Store has thousands to choose from, and most are free.

To browse podcasts, find Podcasts in the black navigation bar at the top of any iTunes Store page, and click its down arrow. A menu of genres appears; click the one you want to browse. Or you can go to the Podcasts home page and click any of the Podcast Quick Links on the right.

When you find a podcast that interests you, click it to open its page. From here, you can preview an episode (just like you would preview a song), download an individual episode, or subscribe to the podcast. When you subscribe, iTunes starts you with the most recent episode and automatically checks for and downloads future episodes.

When you preview a podcast episode in the iTunes Store, you get to listen to about to about 90 seconds' worth of the episode.

When you subscribe to a podcast, your iTunes Library Podcasts section shows a list (in List and Album List views) of your subscriptions, as shown in Figure 3.10. To see a podcast's episodes, click the arrow to the left of the podcast's name. If you want to listen to back episodes, click Get for the episodes you want. To download all back episodes, click the Get All button to the right of the podcast's name.

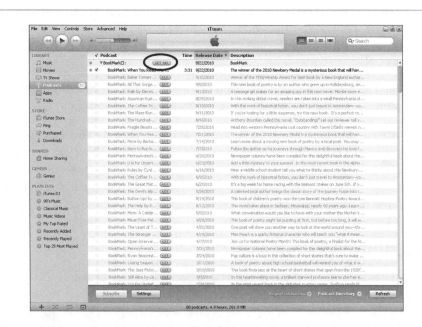

Figure 3.10   *To download all back episodes of a podcast you subscribe to, click Get All (circled).*

ⓒ *Now that you've downloaded some podcasts, learn how to work with them; **see** "Managing Podcasts" (in Chapter 4).*

Buying Apps

An *app* is a program that runs on your iPod Touch, iPhone, or iPad. You can download apps directly to the portable device where you'll use it—this is the easiest way to get an app, and you can begin using it as soon as the download finishes.

🅖 **See** *"Buying Directly Through Your iPod Touch, iPhone, or iPad," coming up in this chapter, to find out how to buy apps directly through one of these devices.*

If you prefer, you can also download an app to your computer from the iTunes Store. When you do that, the next time you sync your iPhone or other device with your computer, the app transfers to the device.

Buying an app via your computer is like buying anything else from the iTunes Store—find the item you want, click its Buy button, sign in (if prompted), confirm, and start the download. Apps are stored in your iTunes Library's Apps section, as shown in Figure 3.11.

Figure 3.11   *The Apps section of the iTunes Library, shown here in Grid view*

Finding Free Content

They say the best things in life are free, right? After all, you got iTunes for free, so how about some free content, too?

The iTunes Store makes it easy for you to find free content in most of its categories. Just go to the home page of the kind of content you want and find its free section:

- **Music**—In the Music Quick Links section on the right, click the Free on iTunes link.

- **Movies**—Scroll down the page to the Free on iTunes section and click See All to peruse your options.

- **TV Shows**—Go to the TV Shows Quick Links section on the right and click Free TV Episodes.

- **Apps**—In the Apps Quick Links section, click Great Free Apps to open a page with hand-picked lists of free apps: New & Noteworthy and Our Favorites. Click See All in either section to browse free apps. Beyond the iTunes Store, you can find free apps at Free App a Day (www.freeappaday.com), which—as its name suggests—offers one free app every day, and at Free App Alert (www.freeappalert.com), which advertises apps that formerly cost money but are now free, whether temporarily or permanently.

If you're browsing the App Store directly from your iPhone or other compatible device, click Categories (at the bottom of the screen) and select the category you're interested in, such as Games or Social Networking. Select a subcategory, if relevant. When you see a list of apps, look at the top of the screen and tap the Top Free tab. This shows the most-downloaded free apps in that category.

- **Podcasts**—Most podcasts are free of charge, so there's no special Free section here.

- **Audiobooks**—These recorded books are expensive to produce, so don't expect freebies here. You can listen to a brief preview for free, but that's about it.

Even though you won't find a Free Audiobooks section in the iTunes Store, you may be able to borrow audiobooks—for free—from your local library. Many libraries have partnered with services such as NetLibrary and OverDrive Digital Media to loan out audiobooks that you can play on your iPod, iPhone, or iPad. You can typically borrow an audiobook for two to three weeks—just make sure the book you want is in iPod-compatible format.

Visit your local library's website to find out if it lends audiobooks. Or go to OverDrive's website (www.overdrive.com) and enter your zip code to search for a participating library near you.

- **iTunes U**—Everything here is free, so browse, enjoy, and be edified!

Creating a Wish List

As you browse the iTunes Store, you'll probably come across songs, albums, videos, and other items that you *think* you want to buy, but you're not ready to plunk down the cash just yet. Yet you want to make sure you can find the item again. That's what a Wish List is for. Your Wish List gathers together items that you've saved to consider buying later.

You don't have to do anything to set up your iTunes Store Wish List; just add items as you come across them. Read on to learn how.

Unlike some other online stores, such as Amazon.com, your iTunes Store Wish List is just for you—it's not made public. Of course, if you know someone else's Apple ID and password (some parents make this a condition of their kids' access to the iTunes Store), you can sign in to that person's account and see his or her Wish List.

 SHOW ME   Media 3.4—Creating and Using an iTunes Store Wish List
Access this video file through your registered Web Edition at
my.safaribooksonline.com/9780132660273/media.

Adding Items to Your Wish List

You can add albums, individual songs, movies, and TV episodes or series to your Wish List. From the product's details page, click the down arrow to the right of the Buy button. A context menu appears, as shown in Figure 3.12; select Add to Wish List. iTunes puts the item on your Wish List.

Figure 3.12   *Adding an item to your iTunes Store Wish List*

Looking at Your Wish List

When you want to look over your Wish List, perhaps to buy an item you stored there, start on the iTunes Store home page. In the Quick Links section, click the My Wish List link. (The number next to the link tells you how many items you currently have on your Wish List.) This opens a My Wish List page like the one shown in Figure 3.13. From here, you have the following options:

- **Find a particular item**—To locate an item that you've saved to your Wish List, go to the section where the item belongs (Albums, Movies, Songs, and so on). Items appear in the order in which you added them, with the earliest items first. Click the section's Sort By drop-down list on the right to choose a different sort method: Besides sorting by date added, you can sort by name, best-sellers, or release date.

- **Go to an item's page**—Want to take another look before you buy? Point your cursor at the cover art, and you'll see an *i* appear in the lower-right corner. When you see that *i*, click the cover to go to the item's product page.

- **Preview a song or TV episode**—To listen to a sample of an individual song or episode that you've added to your list, click its Preview button.

- **Buy an item**—You can buy any item right from your Wish List. Just click its Buy button and proceed with the transaction as usual.

- **Buy all the items on your Wish List**—Feeling extravagant? You can buy your entire Wish List in one swoop by clicking the upper-right Buy All button. This button displays the total price for all the items on your list so that you know how much you're spending before you buy.

- **Delete an item**—If you decide that you don't want an item after all, hover over the cover art (for an album, movie, or TV series) or the individual song or episode. A circled *x* appears: For a full-length item, it's in the upper-left corner of the cover art; for an individual song or episode, it's at the far right of the track list. Click the *x* to remove the item from your Wish List.

Figure 3.13   *A Wish List*

Giving Music or Video as a Gift

You'll probably use the iTunes Store for the occasional self-indulgent splurge, but you can also spread the love by giving others the gift of music or entertainment through iTunes. This section explains how to give an iTunes gift, set up a monthly iTunes allowance, and—when someone returns the favor—redeem a gift card or certificate in the iTunes Store.

Buying an iTunes Gift Card or Gift Certificate

When you give a gift card or certificate, you never have to worry that you bought the wrong size or that your taste and the recipient's don't mesh. iTunes offers two kinds of spend-as-you-wish gifts:

- **Gift card**—A plastic card that you can wrap up or slip into a greeting card

- **Gift certificate**—An iTunes Store credit that you can email to the recipient or print and hand over yourself

With an iTunes gift card, the recipient can select any item from the iTunes Store. Prepaid iTunes gift cards come in denominations of $15, $25, $50, and $100. You can purchase a gift card from the online Apple Store (http://store.apple.com), at any walk-in Apple Retail Store, at many other retailers, or right from the iTunes Store.

> To find an Apple Retail Store near you, go to www.apple.com/retail, enter your city and state or zip code, and then click Locate.

If an approaching birthday or other occasion has slipped your mind, a gift certificate is a handy last-minute gift. You can send the gift certificate to the recipient by email, or you can print a copy, complete with a personal message, from your own printer.

 LET ME TRY IT

Buying a Gift Card from the iTunes Store

You buy the gift card through the Apple Store (which sells a wide variety of Apple products, not just music and video), but you can start the process right from the iTunes Store. Here's how:

1. On the iTunes Store's home page, click Buy iTunes Gifts in the Quick Links section.

2. Scroll down to the gift card section and click Buy Now.

3. Click the image that shows the gift card design and amount you want to buy.

4. Select the number of gift cards you want to buy from the Choose Quantity drop-down list. If you want, type a message to the recipient that will be printed on the card holder. Click Add to Cart.

5. If you want, you can do some more shopping in the Apple Store. When you're done, click Check Out Now.

6. Sign in to the Apple Store using your Apple ID and password (the same ones you use to sign in to iTunes). Click Sign In.

7. Enter the shipping information that tells Apple where to send your gift and choose a shipping method. Click Continue.

> If you're buying a gift card as a one-time gift, you probably don't want to save the recipient's address as your default shipping address at the Apple Store. Make sure that the check box labeled Save As My Default Shipping Information is *un*checked before you proceed.

8. Fill in your payment information as needed. Click Continue.

9. Check your order to make sure everything is correct. Click Place Order Now.

Apple processes your payment information, accepts the order, and emails you a receipt. Your gift card is on its way!

 LET ME TRY IT

Buying a Gift Certificate from the iTunes Store

If you're buying a gift certificate to email or print yourself, follow these steps:

1. On the iTunes Store home page, click Buy iTunes Gifts in the Quick Links section.

2. Choose the kind of gift you want to purchase—email gift certificate or printable gift certificate—and click its Buy Now link.

3a. If you're buying an email gift certificate, enter the recipient's name and email address, the amount of your gift, and a personal message. Click Continue.

3b. If you're buying a printable gift certificate, enter the recipient's name, the amount of your gift, and a personal message. Click Continue.

4. Sign in to your iTunes account and click Continue.

5. Check that the purchase information is correct, and then click Buy.

6a. If you bought an email gift certificate, iTunes sends your gift to the recipient using the email address you supplied.

6b.   If you bought a printable gift certificate, iTunes displays the certificate, complete with your gift message, the date of purchase, and a certificate code. Click Print Now to send the gift certificate to your printer.

> After you've bought a gift certificate, you can view your purchase on your iTunes Account page. So if something goes wrong with your printer or your email gets lost in cyberspace, you can retrieve the information and try again.
>
> To see a gift certificate (or any item) you've purchased in the iTunes Store, click your Apple ID (that's your email address) in the upper-right part of any iTunes Store page. Supply your password, if asked. On your Apple Account Information page, click Purchase History. On the Purchase History page, click the gift certificate to view its information—including the all-important certificate code that allows the recipient to buy stuff in the iTunes Store.

Giving Your Kids an iTunes Allowance

Kids love iTunes and would spend the entire household budget downloading songs, videos, and apps if they could. You can keep a handle on their spending—and keep your credit card information to yourself—by setting up a monthly iTunes allowance. Each month, iTunes charges your account and deposits a predetermined amount of money into the other person's account. iTunes credits the account on the first day of each month until you cancel the allowance.

To get an iTunes allowance, the recipient needs an iTunes account. But don't worry—you can set one up, if necessary, when you set up the allowance.

    LET ME TRY IT

Setting Up an iTunes Store Allowance

Here's how to create a monthly allowance for another iTunes account:

1.   On the iTunes Store's home page, click Buy iTunes Gifts in the Quick Links section.

2.   In the Allowances section, click Set Up an Allowance Now to open the page shown in Figure 3.14.

3.   Fill in the information to set up the account:

    The recipient's name

    How much you want the monthly allowance to be, from $10 to $50

When you want to send the first installment: now or on the first day of next month

The recipient's iTunes account (you need to know the Apple ID the recipient uses to sign in to iTunes)

An optional personal message to include when iTunes notifies the recipient of the allowance

When you've done all that, click Continue.

4. If prompted, sign in to your iTunes account; click Setup.

5. If you're creating a new account for the recipient, fill in the information Apple needs to set up the account: the recipient's email address, name, and birth date, and a password. Click Create to set up the account.

6. Whether you're using an existing account or you've just set up a new one, confirm the information you submitted and click Buy.

iTunes sets up the allowance and sends a notification email to the lucky recipient of your generosity. From here, you can set up another allowance if you want, or click Done to return to the iTunes Gifts page.

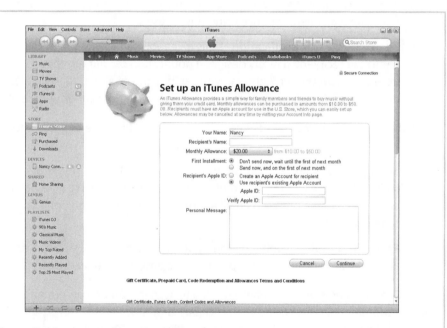

Figure 3.14 *Setting up an iTunes allowance*

Kids grow up and get jobs, and yours won't need an allowance from you forever. To cancel an existing allowance, head to your Apple Account Information page: Click your Apple ID on the right side of the black navigation bar, sign in if prompted, and click the Manage Allowances button. From here, you can temporarily suspend the allowance (maybe until grades improve) or remove it from your account, ending the monthly payments.

Giving Music or Video

If you know exactly the album or video you want to give, you can buy the item and have it sent directly to the recipient's iTunes account so that he or she gets a great surprise when opening iTunes next.

First, browse or search to find the item you want to give. From its product page, click the down arrow to the right of its Buy button. A context menu appears; click Gift This Item. (Instead of the word *item*, you'll see the kind of item you're buying, such as *album* or *movie*.) The Give a Gift page opens (see Figure 3.15).

You have two options for how to deliver an iTunes gift:

- **Via email**—This sends a notification to the gift's recipient and tells where the new item in his or her iTunes account came from. You can send the same gift to multiple recipients at once using this method.

- **By printing a gift notification**—This gives you something physical to present to the recipient: a nicely designed notification of your gift that you print from your own printer. Although you can buy the same gift for several people using this method, you have to buy and print each notification separately.

Pick the method your want for delivering your gift and fill in the required information:

- **Send gift via email**—When you turn on this radio button, iTunes asks for the recipient's name and email address. (To send the gift to more than one recipient, put a comma between email addresses.) You can add an optional message, if you want.

- **Print gift myself**—Turning on this radio button changes the screen so that all you have to fill in is the recipient's name and an optional message.

Click Continue and sign in if iTunes asks you to. Confirm that the information you've submitted is correct, and then click Buy Gift. Now the next time the recipient signs in to iTunes, your gift downloads to his or her iTunes device.

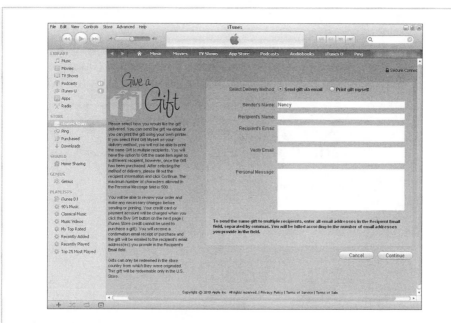

Figure 3.15 *Giving a gift through the iTunes Store*

Redeeming an iTunes Gift Card or Certificate

It may be better to give than to receive—but receiving sure is fun, too. When someone gives you an iTunes gift card or certificate, you can redeem it by going to the iTunes Store home page and clicking Redeem under Quick Links. This opens the Redeem Code page shown in Figure 3.16.

In the Redeem Code box, type in the code that's printed on your gift card or certificate—upper- versus lowercase letters don't matter. (If you received the certificate via email, you can simply copy the code and paste it into the box.) Click the Redeem button.

iTunes asks you to sign in to your account, so do that now. Click Redeem. iTunes credits your account with the amount you were given; any credit you have appears in the black bar above the screen, to the left of the email address you use as your Apple ID.

The next time you buy something, Apple applies the credit toward your purchase. So if you have a $10 credit and you buy an album for $10.99, for example, Apple puts your $10 credit toward the purchase and then charges your credit card just 99 cents.

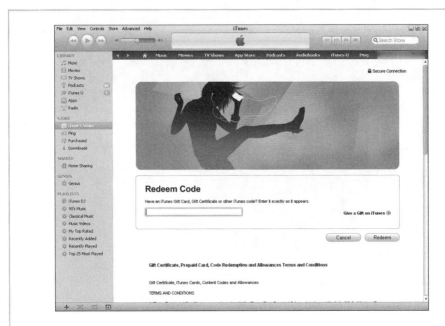

Figure 3.16 *Redeeming a gift card or certificate*

Buying Directly Through Your iPod Touch, iPhone, or iPad

When you use your computer to buy items in the iTunes Store, iTunes downloads those items to your computer and then syncs with your iPod, iPhone, or iPad the next time you connect one of those devices to the computer's USB port.

But you're not always sitting in front of your computer. Sometimes you want to download music and video directly to your iPod so you have on-the-go entertainment. Imagine that you're out at a club, for example, listening to a great new band, and you want to get the album so you can listen again on the way home. You're nowhere near your computer, but you want to buy the album *now*.

If you have an iPod Touch, iPhone, or iPad, Apple makes that easy, because an iTunes Store app comes preloaded on your device. First, make sure that your device is connected to a Wi-Fi or 3G network. Then just tap the iTunes icon to go straight to the iTunes store (see Figure 3.17).

Figure 3.17   *The mobile iTunes Store (shown here on an iPhone)*

The first time you access the iTunes Store from your portable device, it opens to the Music page. Here you can browse new releases, top 10 lists, or your favorite genres. Tap the button you want at the top of the screen to see what's new. Use these buttons at the bottom of the screen to navigate the site:

- **Music**—All your favorite hits in all your favorite genres are here. The New Releases page shows featured items, like the free single of the week.

- **Videos**—Browse the latest movies, TV shows, and music videos here.

- **Ping**—After you've signed up for Ping in iTunes, you can access this music-based social networking site from your portable device.

G *To find out how to get started with Ping,* **see** *"Turning on Ping and Creating Your Profile" in Chapter 10. To learn about using Ping with your iPod Touch, iPhone, or iPad,* **see** *"Going Mobile with Ping" (also in Chapter 10).*

- **Search**—If you're looking for a specific artist or title, you can search from here.

- **More**—Tap this button to find ringtones, podcasts, audiobooks, or iTunes U offerings. You can also see what you've purchased in the Downloads section.

When you see an item you want to buy, tap the item to see a mobile version of its product page, like the one shown in Figure 3.18. From here, you can read reviews, listen to or watch previews, and buy or rent the item.

Figure 3.18   *A product page (for an album) in the mobile iTunes Store*

Buying a Song or Album

When you've found a piece of music that you want to buy, open its product page. (Figure 3.18 shows an example.) If you want to preview a song, touch its number in the track list. The number flips around and turns into a play indicator—quick, plug in your ear buds, because the preview lasts only about 30 seconds.

To buy the song (or a whole album), touch the button that shows its price. The price button morphs into a Buy button. Touch it again, and, if prompted, sign in to your iTunes account. As soon as you've signed in, the download begins. (Tap More, at the bottom of the screen, and then Downloads, if you want to watch its progress.) You can play your new song or album as soon as it's fully downloaded to your device.

The next time you connect your device to your computer, the item you bought in the mobile iTunes Store gets downloaded to your computer's iTunes library during the sync.

Buying or Renting a Movie, TV Show, or Music Video

Just as you can on the iTunes website, you can preview many videos before you buy in the mobile iTunes Store. When you find a video that interests you, open its product page and tap the Preview button. Your device turns into a video viewer, as shown in Figure 3.19, and shows the film's trailer.

Like what you saw? Tap Done to go back to the product page. Touch the video's Rent or Buy button. The button changes to read Buy Now or Rent Now. Touch it again, sign in to your iTunes account, and make your purchase.

Figure 3.19   *Previewing a movie on an iPhone*

After you get some music in your iTunes library, you'll want to listen to it. This chapter shows you how to get the best listening experience from iTunes.

4

Listening in iTunes

Even the biggest music library isn't much use if there's no way to hear its treasures. This chapter is all about using iTunes as an audio player. It starts with the basics: how to listen to music (whether you're playing a CD or music that's stored in your iTunes library), Internet radio shows, audiobooks, and podcasts. You'll learn ways to optimize your listening experience, including how to use the iTunes Equalizer for the best-quality sound, set up crossfading between songs, and use the right settings for audiobooks. And if listening to music is fun, watching it can be even better—read all about the iTunes Visualizer, which creates pulsing patterns in time to your music.

Listening to Music and More in iTunes

Even if you don't have an iPod, you can use iTunes to listen to music through your computer. And music is the just the beginning—you can listen to audiobooks and podcasts, too. Whatever you're in the mood to hear, this section gets you started.

Authorizing Your Computer to Play iTunes Purchases

To protect copyrights, many of your iTunes Store purchases will play only on an authorized computer. This makes sure that copyrighted works get distributed in a way that's fair to the copyright holders—the artists, authors, and producers who bring you your entertainment.

You can authorize a computer with just a couple of clicks: Select Store, Authorize This Computer. In the dialog box that opens, sign in with your Apple ID and password, and then click Authorize. Apple checks your login info and authorizes the computer. You'll see a confirmation message telling you that the authorization was successful and how many computers are authorized for your account. Click OK to close the message.

The computer on which you set up your iTunes Store account is automatically authorized to play your purchases.

Your iTunes Store account can have up to five authorized computers associated with it. Any of those five computers can play the content you buy in the iTunes Store—but no more than those five. So if you've already authorized five computers and you want to play your iTunes Store purchases on a different computer, you have to deauthorize one of the currently authorized computers before you can add the new one.

For example, if you've authorized iTunes on your laptop, along with those of your spouse and all three kids, that's five authorized computers. If you want to play music through the desktop computer in the family room because it's hooked up to high-quality speakers, you'll have to deauthorize one of the laptops before you can authorize the family-room computer to play your iTunes purchases.

To deauthorize a computer, select Store, Deauthorize This Computer. Sign in with your Apple ID and password, and click Deauthorize. Apple removes the authorization from that computer; now you can authorize a different one.

For the purpose of authorization, iPods, iPhones, and iPads don't count as computers. You don't have to authorize those devices, and playing your iTunes purchases on them doesn't limit the number of computers you can use to play those purchases.

Listening to Music in Your iTunes Library

When you're in the mood for a song or an album that you've stored in iTunes, listening to it is easy, as this section shows.

 LET ME TRY IT

Playing a Song from Your iTunes Library

To listen to the tunes you've stored in your iTunes library, follow these quick steps:

1. In iTunes, click Music in the left source list. If you want to play one of your playlists, find it in the source list's Playlists section.

2. Find the album, song, or playlist you want to listen to. Click to select it.

3. To play a song, you can either double-click its title or click the Play button (see Figure 4.1) in the iTunes controls at the top of your screen.

iTunes plays the song you selected and continues playing songs in sequence (unless you've told iTunes to shuffle the songs).

Ⓖ *To learn about Shuffle mode in iTunes,* ***see*** *"Shuffling Songs" (later in this chapter).*

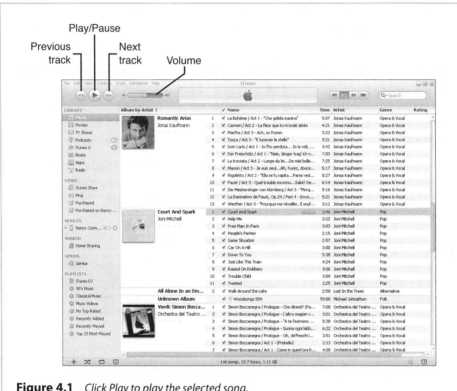

Figure 4.1   *Click Play to play the selected song.*

Ⓖ *iTunes offers a couple of alternative players. To check out these alternatives,* ***see*** *"Using the iTunes Mini Player" and "Using the iTunes Desktop Player" (both in Chapter 11, "iTunes Tips and Tricks").*

Playing an Album from Your iTunes Library

If you're in the mood to listen to one of the albums you've stored in iTunes, simply find the album you want and play its first song. After that song has played, the next begins—and so on, throughout the album.

If you're in a view that displays album artwork—Album List, Grid, or Cover Flow—double-click the album cover to play the album.

If iTunes is in Shuffle mode (you'll read more about that later in this chapter), it won't play your album's songs in order. To hear an album from start to finish, make sure the status bar's Shuffle button is gray, not blue (click to toggle the button on and off).

Listening to a CD

If you're going to be using iTunes primarily to play CDs that you insert into your computer, first make sure that you have iTunes set up so that it won't automatically import CD tracks. To make sure iTunes won't start ripping tracks from your CD as soon as you insert the disc, select Edit, Preferences (on a PC) or iTunes, Preferences (on a Mac). On the General tab of the dialog box that opens, make one of these selections from the When You Insert a CD drop-down list:

- **Show CD**—This option adds the CD to your source list (under Devices) and lists its tracks, but it doesn't play or import the CD.

- **Begin Playing**—This is the best option if you want to use iTunes primarily as a CD player.

- **Ask to Import CD**—When you choose this option (it's the default), iTunes asks whether you want to import the CD you've inserted. You can play the CD instead by clicking No.

🄶 *To learn more about the settings you can choose for inserting a CD, **see** "Adjusting Your CD Import Settings" (in Chapter 2, "Getting Content into iTunes").*

After you've set up iTunes so that it won't automatically import CDs you insert, playing a CD is simple. If you've set Begin Playing as the default way to handle CDs, all you have to do is put the CD in your computer's CD/DVD drive. When you shut the drawer, iTunes starts (if it's not open already) and plays your CD.

If you've set iTunes to show the CD but do nothing else, the CD appears under Devices in the source list, and iTunes shows the CD's tracks in List view, as shown in Figure 4.2. Double-click any track to play it. iTunes plays the tracks in order (unless you've set it to Shuffle mode), starting with the one you selected.

🄶 ***See** "Shuffling Songs," coming up in this chapter, to learn about Shuffle mode in iTunes.*

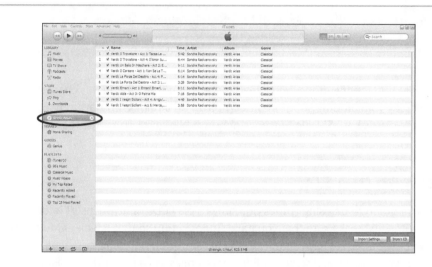

Figure 4.2   *Inserted CDs appear in List view, under Devices (circled).*

If the iTunes settings make it ask before it imports a CD, inserting a CD brings up a dialog box that asks you to confirm that you want to import the CD. If you just want to play the CD, click No. iTunes shows the CD under Devices and its track list, as in Figure 4.2. Double-click the track you want to start with.

If you have iTunes set to import CDs automatically whenever you insert them, you can still just listen, if you prefer. When you insert the CD and the import begins, just click the lower-right Stop Importing button. iTunes stops the import, and the screen looks like the one in Figure 4.2. Now you can listen to your CD instead of ripping it.

Using the Playback Controls

The upper-left playback controls, shown in Figure 4.1, let you work with the currently selected song. They look just like the controls on a CD or DVD player, so their functions shouldn't be a big surprise. Here's what the playback controls do:

- **Previous Track**—Plays the track before the one currently playing. If you just listened to a song and you want to "play it again, Sam," click this.

- **Play/Pause**—This button changes to reflect the status of the current selection. If the button shows a triangle, it's the Play button; click it to play the selected song. If the button shows two vertical lines, it's the Pause button; click it to stop playing the current song. (If you click Play again, the song picks up at the point where you paused it.)

- **Next Track**—Plays the track after the one currently playing. Not in the mood for the song you're hearing? Click this button to skip to the next one.

- **Volume**—Controls the volume. Move the slider to the right to crank up the volume; move it left to quiet things down.

Listening to Internet Radio

Internet radio stations stream their programs over the Internet so that you can listen through your computer. Whether you like to catch an occasional show or have radio streaming in the background all day, you can use iTunes to listen to your favorite Internet radio programs.

SHOW ME   Media 4.1—iTunes Radio Stations
Access this video file through your registered Web Edition at
my.safaribooksonline.com/9780132660273/media.

LET ME TRY IT

Finding and Listening to an Internet Radio Station

When you want to listen to an Internet radio program, follow these steps:

1. In the iTunes source list, click Radio (under Library).

2. A list of genres opens, as shown in Figure 4.3. To see the stations belonging to a genre, click the triangle beside the genre's name.

3. Find the station you want to listen to and double-click its name. iTunes connects to the station and plays what it's streaming right now. As you listen, the Status pane displays the station's name and a timer that shows how long you've been listening.

4. When you're done listening, click the Pause button in your iTunes controls to stop the stream. You can also switch to a different station by double-clicking its name.

Figure 4.3 *Choosing an Internet radio station*

If you want a radio show that doesn't appear in the iTunes list, you can listen by telling iTunes where to get the broadcast. Copy the show's web address (it'll look something like this example: http://www.station.com/show/example.mp3) to your computer's Clipboard. In iTunes, select Advanced, Open Audio Stream. In the dialog box that opens, paste in the show's web address and click OK. iTunes gets the show and plays it for you.

Listening to Audiobooks

Audiobooks are a great way to get some reading in while you're doing something else, like tidying up the house or making dinner. You can listen to audiobooks through your iPod, of course, but you can also play them right from your iTunes library.

iTunes can play audiobooks that you buy through the iTunes Store or from Audible.com (www.audible.com). Each site has slightly different conditions for using audiobooks:

- **iTunes Store**—When you buy an audiobook from the iTunes Store, you can download it on up to five authorized computers at a time for playback, just as with any other iTunes Store purchase. Audiobooks from the iTunes Store end with the file extension .m4b.

Ⓒ *To find out how to authorize and deauthorize computers to play the content you buy in the iTunes Store, **see** "Authorizing Your Computer to Play iTunes Purchases" (earlier in this chapter).*

- **Audible.com**—If you buy an audiobook from Audible.com, you can download it to a maximum of three authorized computers at a time. These audiobook files end with the file extension .aa or .aax.

Playing an audiobook is just like playing music. In the left iTunes source list, click Books (under Library). Select the book you want to listen to, and double-click it or click the Play button.

Ⓒ *To learn how to optimize iTunes settings for listening to audiobooks, **see** "Selecting the Best Settings for Audiobooks," later in this chapter.*

Managing Podcasts

Whether you subscribe to your favorite can't-miss-'em podcasts or just listen to an occasional episode, you need to manage the podcasts you keep in your iTunes library. This section describes how to tell iTunes when to check for new episodes, what to do with old episodes, and more.

Ⓒ *To find out how to add podcasts to your iTunes library, **see** "Subscribing to a Podcast Through iTunes" (in Chapter 2) and "Subscribing to Podcasts" (in Chapter 3, "Shopping in the iTunes Store").*

 LET ME TRY IT

Choosing Podcast Settings

iTunes gives you a lot of flexibility in how it handles podcasts. You can specify how often it checks for new episodes, what to do when new episodes are available, and what to do with episodes you've already downloaded. It's all up to you.

To adjust your podcast settings, follow these steps:

1. In your iTunes library, click Podcasts to see a list of the podcasts you subscribe to.

2. Select the podcast whose settings you want to adjust.

3. At the bottom of the iTunes window, click the Settings button to open the dialog box shown in Figure 4.4.

4a. Make a selection from the Check for New Episodes drop-down list. You can tell iTunes to check for new episodes hourly, daily (the default), or weekly, or to wait until you tell it to check.

4b. The Settings For drop-down list shows the podcast you selected. If you want, you can select a different podcast. Choose Podcast Defaults if you want these settings to apply to all your podcasts.

4c. If you want to adjust the default settings for downloading and keeping podcast episodes, make sure the Use Default Settings check box is *un*checked. This makes the two drop-down lists beneath it active.

4d. In the When New Episodes Are Available drop-down list, choose what you want iTunes to do when it checks and finds a new episode: download all new episodes (there may be several if you haven't checked in a while), download only the most recent episode (leaving any older ones on the site, even if you haven't listened to them), or do nothing (wait for you to refresh the episodes yourself).

4e. Use the Episodes to Keep drop-down list to manage how long iTunes hangs on to downloaded episodes. You can save all episodes, only those you haven't yet listened to, only the most recent episode, or up to 10 of the most recent episodes.

5. When you've set things up the way you want them, click OK to put your new settings to work.

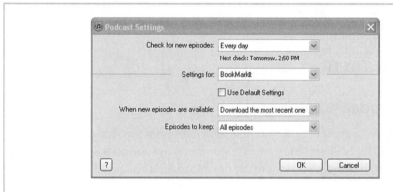

Figure 4.4 *Picking your podcast settings*

Checking for New Episodes

If you're eagerly awaiting the next episode in your favorite podcast, you can tell iTunes to check for it right now. In your iTunes library, click Podcasts and then click the lower-right Refresh button. iTunes checks for new episodes and downloads any it finds, according to your settings.

Click the Refresh button to check for new episodes after you've told iTunes that you want to do this manually in your podcast settings.

Unsubscribing from a Podcast

If a certain podcast just doesn't interest you anymore, you can stop subscribing to it. In your iTunes library, click Podcasts and select the podcast that you no longer want to update. Click the lower-left Unsubscribe button.

iTunes keeps the podcast in your list, but it will no longer get new episodes. You can resume your subscription whenever you like: Just find the podcast in your library and click the Subscribe button to the right of its name.

🔄 *Unsubscribing doesn't delete the podcasts or its episodes from your library; to do that, **see** the next section.*

Deleting a Podcast or Episode

When you delete a podcast from your iTunes library, that podcast also disappears from any portable device that you sync with your library. So if you think you might want to listen to the episode on your iPod the next time you go jogging, wait to delete it.

To delete a single podcast episode, find the particular episode you want to delete and right-click it (on a PC) or Ctrl-click it (on a Mac). From the context menu, select Delete. iTunes asks whether you're sure you want to remove the episode from your library. Click Remove. Next, iTunes asks what to do with the file after it's removed from your iTunes library:

- **Move to Recycle Bin/Trash**—Click this button if you want to delete the episode from your computer. The next time you empty this folder, it's gone.

- **Keep File**—Click this button if you want to keep the episode in your iTunes Media folder. Even though it no longer appears in your library, you can find the episode again with a bit of digging.

You can delete multiple podcast episodes at once. Hold down the Shift key to select adjacent episodes, or the Ctrl or Cmd key to select noncontiguous episodes.

You can delete an entire podcast—including all its episodes—using the same method. Instead of selecting an episode to delete, however, select the whole podcast and then proceed as just described.

Optimizing Your Audio Experience

To get the most out of listening in iTunes, you can adjust its settings to enhance your music, bringing out richer tones, as this section explains. And because iTunes is about more than just music, this section also shows you how to choose the best settings for your audiobooks.

Making Your Tunes Sound Better with the iTunes Equalizer

Not all music is created equal—the Big Band tunes your parents swing-dance to sound different from the hiphop your kids prefer, the classical music the city symphony plays, and good old-fashioned rock-n-roll. You can adjust the iTunes settings to get the best sound for the music you're listening to. That's what the iTunes Equalizer is for. The Equalizer, shown in Figure 4.5, lets you adjust the amount of bass, treble, and frequencies in between to make your music sound its best. Select View, Show Equalizer (in Windows) or Window, Equalizer (on a Mac) to see it.

What's an Equalizer?

In a nutshell, an equalizer is a set of 10 volume controls, as you can see in Figure 4.5. Different sounds have different frequencies—that is, different vibrational rates. Deeper, lower-pitched sounds vibrate more slowly than high-pitched ones, which vibrate very fast. Sound frequencies are measured in hertz (Hz).

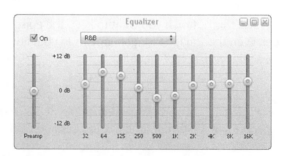

Figure 4.5 *Adjusting frequencies with the iTunes Equalizer*

In an equalizer, each slider controls the volume of one-tenth of the audio spectrum—the sounds that can be heard by the human ear—from 32Hz at the low end to 16,000Hz at the high end. You can use the equalizer to adjust the volumes of these different frequencies to balance the sound of a song. You can do this by hand, or you can use one of the iTunes presets to get the best sound (Figure 4.5 is optimized for R&B). The next sections tell you how.

> To use the Equalizer, make sure there's a check mark in its upper-left On check box.

 SHOW ME   Media 4.2—Using the iTunes Equalizer
Access this video file through your registered Web Edition at
my.safaribooksonline.com/9780132660273/media.

Choosing an Equalizer Preset

If you want to optimize the sound for a particular kind of music, iTunes already knows the best equalizer settings for that genre. You can choose a preset in two ways:

- **From the File menu**—Select File, Get Info, and then click the Options tab. Click the Equalizer Preset drop-down list and select the preset for the kind of music you want. Click OK to apply the preset.

- **From the Equalizer**—If you have the Equalizer open (choose View, Show Equalizer to bring it up), click the drop-down list near the top of the box to choose a preset. The sliders move to show the settings for the preset you picked.

If you're playing a song when you choose a preset, the playback automatically reflects your choice, so you can hear how the preset affects its sound. If you're not currently playing the song, the preset will apply to the song the next time iTunes plays it.

> After you've selected a preset, you can fine-tune its settings by adjusting the Equalizer's individual volume controls. To change them back to the defaults, just select the original preset again. If you adjust an existing preset's settings, save your version as a new preset (keep reading to find out how to do that).

Adjusting the Equalizer Manually

The iTunes Equalizer presets are a convenient way to get the best sound for different kinds of music, but you can also adjust the Equalizer by hand to get exactly the mix of sound you want. For any frequency, move the slider upward to increase that frequency's volume; move downward to make the frequency quieter.

Increasing the volume in the 32Hz–64Hz range boosts the bass; move the 125Hz slider upward to bring out warm tones, such as those from cellos. At the other end of the frequency range—say, 8,000Hz and 16,000Hz—you brighten higher tones, such as those from flutes and violins. Experiment to see what mix sounds best to your ear.

Preamp volume, the control on the Equalizer's left side, applies equally to all frequencies. So if you move the Preamp slider up 3 decibels, for example, you increase the volume of each frequency by that amount. Preamp volume makes the song louder or softer without changing the balance of frequencies.

Creating Your Own Preset

If you create a sound mix you like, you don't have to write down the settings to remember them—you can save them and apply them to other songs by creating your own preset. After you've done some manual adjustment of the volume controls, click the Equalizer's preset drop-down list (it'll say Manual) and select New Preset.

The Make Preset dialog box opens; type a name for your new preset and then click OK. iTunes saves your Equalizer settings and adds them to your list of presets, using the name you specified.

Managing Presets

To delete or rename a preset, click the Equalizer's drop-down menu and select Edit List. A dialog box similar to the one shown in Figure 4.6 opens, listing your presets. Select a preset to take one of the following actions:

- **Give the preset a new name**—Click Rename to open the Rename dialog box. Type the preset's new name and click OK.

- **Remove the preset**—Click Delete. iTunes asks whether you're sure you want to get rid of this preset; click Delete to confirm.

Figure 4.6 *Editing Equalizer presets*

Whether you're renaming or deleting, iTunes asks whether you want the change to apply to all songs currently using that preset. Click Yes or No, as you prefer, and click Done when you're finished managing your presets.

Using the Sound Enhancer

If you don't feel like fiddling with the Equalizer's controls, there's a quicker, easier way to optimize sound in iTunes. The Sound Enhancer doesn't give you the same precise, fine-grained control as the Equalizer, but it boosts music's high and low frequencies, giving depth to the sound.

 LET ME TRY IT

Enhancing Sound

Here's how to use the iTunes Sound Enhancer:

1. Select Edit, Preferences (in Windows) or iTunes, Preferences (on a Mac).

2. Click the Playback tab, shown in Figure 4.7.

3. Check the Sound Enhancer check box.

4. Drag the slider to the right (toward High) to enhance the sound. A setting of High boosts both the high and low frequencies.

5. Click OK to apply sound enhancement.

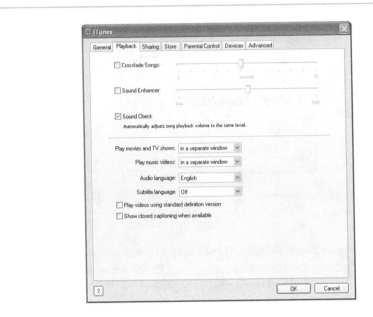

Figure 4.7   *Control sound on the Playback tab*

If you decide that you don't like what the Sound Enhancer does to your songs, you can turn it off. Return to the Playback tab and click the Sound Enhancer check box to remove the check mark. Or you can return the Sound Enhancer slider to its neutral setting, smack in the middle of its range, which has no effect on playback.

Crossfading Between Songs

When you're at a club, dancing to songs played by a DJ, the songs fade smoothly from one into the next. You don't even have to pause for breath between dances. That seamless fade-out/fade-in between songs is called *crossfading*, and you can set it up in iTunes.

 LET ME TRY IT

Setting Up Crossfading

To have the next song fade in as the current one is fading out, do this:

1. Select Edit, Preferences (in Windows) or iTunes, Preferences (on a Mac).

2. Click the Playback tab, shown in Figure 4.7.

3. Click the Crossfade Songs check box.

4. The slider indicates how many seconds crossfade lasts (each tick mark on the scale represents 1 second). Move the slider to the left (toward 1) to decrease crossfade; move the slider to the right (toward 12) to increase crossfade.

5. Click OK to start crossfading songs.

Crossfading during playback works only in iTunes, so this setting won't sync to your iPod, iPhone, or iPad.

Standardizing Volume with Sound Check

Have you ever listened to music and found that you had to turn up the volume to hear one track, but then the next track practically blasted your ears off your head? That's because there's a lot of variation in how songs are recorded and CDs are manufactured. The volume level for different discs (even for different songs on the same disc) can vary significantly.

Whether you prefer window-rattling blasting or quiet background music, you can keep the volume steady for all the songs in your iTunes library.

 LET ME TRY IT

Standardizing Volume

To standardize volume throughout your iTunes library, follow these steps:

1. In the Controls bar at the top of the iTunes screen, drag the volume slider to the volume you want as your standard.

2. Select Edit, Preferences (in Windows) or iTunes, Preferences (on a Mac).

3. Click the Playback tab, shown in Figure 4.7.

4. Click to put a check mark in the Sound Check box.

5. Click OK.

iTunes standardizes the volume for all your songs. (This setting carries over to your portable device when you sync it with iTunes.)

You can turn off Sound Check at any time. Just return to the Playback tab and remove the check mark from the Sound Check box. When you do, the volume of songs reflects how they were recorded.

Selecting the Best Settings for Audiobooks

Audiobooks require some special settings that don't necessarily apply to music—you want to listen to an audiobook's chapters in order, for example (no shuffling), and you want to be able to insert a virtual bookmark so you can pick up right where you left off. Read on to learn more about setting up iTunes for easy audiobook listening.

> The Equalizer isn't just for music. To get the best sound for audiobooks and spoken podcasts, select Spoken Word from the Equalizer's drop-down list of presets.

 **LET ME TRY IT**

Auto-Bookmarking a Track

Imagine that you're sitting on the bus, listening to an audiobook thriller. Right in the middle of an exciting scene, you reach your stop and have to quit listening. When you're ready to pick up the story again, you don't want to start over at the beginning of the chapter—you want to know *now* whether the hero got out of that building before it blew up.

You can tell iTunes to remember where you stopped listening so that when you return to your audiobook, the action picks up exactly where you left off—it's like sticking a bookmark in a physical book. And if you transfer the audiobook between devices—say that you start listening on your iPod and then you sync your iPod with your desktop computer to continue listening at home—the bookmark gets transferred from one device to the other. That way, you never have to lose your place.

Audiobooks that you buy from the iTunes Store or Audible.com automatically remember playback positions, so if that's where you got your audiobooks, you don't have to adjust this setting yourself. (In fact, you can't change it.) But if you've imported some audiobooks from CDs that you own, you'll want to make sure that auto-bookmarking is turned on.

Here's how to set a track so that iTunes remembers the playback position:

1. Select the track you want.

2. Click File, Get Info.

3. In the dialog box that opens, click the Options tab, shown in Figure 4.8.

4. Make sure the Media Kind is Audiobook.

5. Click the box labeled Remember Playback Position.

6. Click OK.

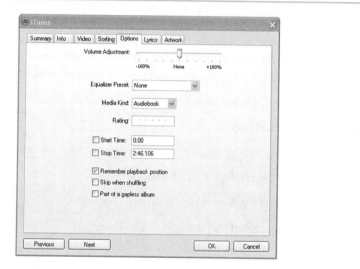

Figure 4.8   *Telling iTunes to remember a track's playback position*

 LET ME TRY IT

Auto-Bookmarking Multiple Tracks

To save time, you can also tell iTunes to remember playback position for multiple tracks:

1. Select the tracks you want. (Hold down the Shift key or the Ctrl/Cmd key to select multiple tracks.)

2. Click File, Get Info.

3. If iTunes asks whether it's okay to edit multiple tracks at once, click Yes.

4. In the dialog box that opens, click the Options tab.

5. Make sure the Media Kind is Audiobook.

6. From the Remember Position drop-down list, select Yes.

7. Click OK to apply the setting to all the tracks you chose.

 LET ME TRY IT

Preventing an Audiobook Track from Shuffling

You don't want to hear audiobook chapters out of order, and you definitely *don't* want Lesson 3 of your Spanish textbook to blast from your speakers in the middle of a party. If you buy audiobooks through the iTunes Store or Audible.com, those books are automatically excluded from shuffle playback. When you've imported an audiobook from a CD, though, you have to do it yourself. Here's how:

1. In your iTunes library, select the track that you *don't* want to shuffle.

2. Select File, Get Info.

3. In the dialog box that opens, click the Options tab (see Figure 4.8).

4. Make sure the Media Kind is Audiobook.

5. Click to select the Skip When Shuffling check box.

6. Click OK to prevent this track from shuffling.

> Although this section is about audiobook tracks, you can use the same steps to keep songs from shuffling. (Just make sure that the Media Kind selection is Music.) That way, that embarrassingly cheesy '70s ballad or that hiphop song whose lyrics are too risqué for dinner with the folks won't start playing unexpectedly.

 LET ME TRY IT

Preventing Multiple Tracks from Shuffling

To exclude multiple tracks from shuffled playback, follow these steps:

1. Select the tracks you want. (Hold down the Shift key or the Ctrl/Cmd key to select multiple tracks.)

2. Click File, Get Info.

3. If iTunes asks whether it's okay to edit multiple tracks at once, click Yes.

4. In the dialog box that opens, click the Options tab.

5. From the Skip When Shuffling drop-down list, select Yes.

6. Click OK, and these tracks won't be shuffled.

Shuffling Songs

Shuffling songs means playing them in random order. Instead of hearing the same old songs in the same old order, shuffling keeps listening fresh.

To put iTunes into Shuffle mode, click the lower-left Shuffle button, shown in Figure 4.9. When you want to hear an album's songs in order, click the button again to stop shuffling. When this button is blue, Shuffle mode is on; when it's gray, Shuffle mode is off.

Shuffle ⏌   ⌐ Repeat

Figure 4.9   *Shuffle and Repeat modes on*

Repeating Songs

To have iTunes repeat all songs in your library or playlist when it's finished playing them, click the Repeat button on the left side of the status bar. (You can see it in Figure 4.9.) When the button is blue, Repeat mode is on; click it again to turn off Repeat mode (the button turns gray).

If you can't get enough of one particular song and you want to hear it over and over (and over and over) again, click the Repeat button once (if Repeat mode is already on) or twice (if Repeat mode is off). The Repeat button turns blue and displays the number 1. The current song will repeat for as long until you click the button again to make it stop.

Rating Your Favorite Tracks

Keep track of your favorite (and least favorite) tracks by rating them. You don't have to rate tracks in iTunes, but if you do, you can sort songs by rating to find your favorites. iTunes automatically adds your highest-rated songs to your My Top Rated playlist so you can listen to just your faves.

To rate a song, select the song in the track list and choose File, Rating. A submenu flies out (see Figure 4.10), letting you pick a rating from one star to five stars. (You can also select None, for no rating.) Click the number of stars you want to give the song, from one (hate it!) to five (love it!).

Figure 4.10   *Rating a song*

You can see a song's rating in its Rating column on the right. Click the column header to sort your music by the ratings you've assigned.

🅖 *Genius uses the ratings you assign tracks to suggest new music you'll love. To learn more about Genius suggestions,* **see** *"Getting Genius Recommendations" (in Chapter 5, "Playing with Playlists").*

Watching Your Music with the iTunes Visualizer

If you want a light show with your music, turn on the iTunes Visualizer, shown in Figure 4.11. The Visualizer creates a hypnotic kaleidoscope of shifting colors and patterns to the beat of the song that's playing. The effects cycle through different modes to create an ever-changing display.

 SHOW ME   Media 4.3—The iTunes Visualizer
Access this video file through your registered Web Edition at
my.safaribooksonline.com/9780132660273/media.

To turn on the Visualizer, select View, Show Visualizer while a song is playing. Your screen erupts with fireworks and moving designs. The current song shows in the lower-left corner and then gradually fades out as the song continues. To make the display take over your entire computer screen, press Ctrl+F (on a PC) or Cmd-F (on a Mac), or select View, Full Screen. The iTunes Control and Status bars disappear, giving the light show free rein. Press Esc (or Ctrl/Cmd-F) to exit full-screen mode.

iTunes has two choices of Visualizer built in:

- **iTunes Visualizer**—This version, first introduced in iTunes 8, is the one shown in Figure 4.11.

- **iTunes Classic Visualizer**—This was the original iTunes Visualizer. It starts you off with the Apple logo, and the show goes from there.

- **Lathe, Jelly, and Stix**—These visualizers became available for Mac users with the release of Mac OS 10.5 Leopard.

To switch between versions of the Visualizer, select View, Visualizer, and then pick either iTunes Visualizer or iTunes Classic Visualizer.

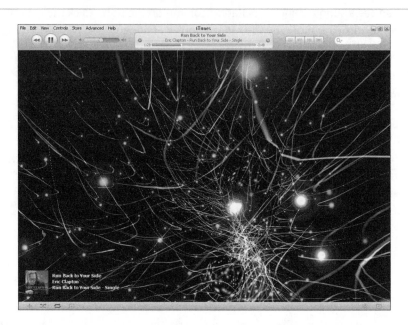

Figure 4.11   *The Visualizer creates a visual display to the beat of the song.*

If you always want the Visualizer to take up the full screen when it plays, you can set that in your preferences. Select Edit, Preferences (on a PC) or iTunes, Preferences (on a Mac), and click the Advanced tab. Put a check in the check box marked Display Full Screen, and then click OK. Now whenever you show the Visualizer, it'll take up the full screen.

To close the Visualizer and go back to the normal iTunes window, select View, Hide Visualizer.

Pressing Ctrl+T (on a PC) or Cmd-T (on a Mac) also toggles the Visualizer on and off.

Customizing the Visualizer

While the Visualizer is playing, you can play with it. The keyboard commands listed in Table 4.1 change the appearance and behavior of the Visualizer as it plays—just press a key to see track information, change the color palette, or cycle through the different effects. Experiment with them to see which you like best.

Table 4.1   Keyboard Commands for the iTunes Visualizer

Key	What It Does	Notes
I	Shows track information	This displays the track name, artist, album, and cover art in the lower-left corner.
M	Changes mode	Changing the mode moves you through the cycle of effects.
P	Changes color palette	This gives the effect a different set of colors.
C	Toggles autocycle	You can turn off automatic cycling through different modes and colors (it's on by default).
F	Toggles freeze mode	This freezes the pattern in its current configuration, while the camera continues to show different angles.
N	Toggles nebula mode	This emphasizes (or deemphasizes) clouds in the background of the pattern.
L	Toggles camera lock	The pattern continues to move, but you see it from a constant angle.
?	Shows/hides Help	When you press ?, the Visualizer's keyboard commands appear in the upper-left part of the screen and then gradually fade out.

Installing a Third-Party Visualizer Plug-In

For even more Visualizer variety, you can download and install third-party plug-ins that change the look of onscreen patterns and pulses. If you use a Mac, take a look at some of these Visualizer plug-ins:

- **Wowlab (www.wowlab.net)**—Click Study and then iTunes Visualizer to see plug-ins that add visual effects, such as Snow, Dragon, and Circle (which lays out the track name, artist, and album in a circular format and rotates it in 3D space). You can watch a video showing a preview of each effect.

- **Digital Media Exploration (http://secd.unl.edu/~mbentz/bentz)**—Click Visualizers to select from three different options.

- **Volcano Kit (http://volcanokit.com)**—This visualizer displays adjustable colored bands that respond to the music.

Windows users have fewer options, but take a look at what's available at Sound Spectrum (www.soundspectrum.com), which has several visualizers available for both PCs and Macs.

After you've downloaded a visualizer plug-in, you have to let iTunes know where to find it. To install a visualizer plug-in, close iTunes and then follow these directions:

- **In Mac OS X 10.5 or higher**—Drag the file included with your download here: *Yourfolder*/Library/iTunes/iTunes Plug-Ins (where *Yourfolder* is the actual name of your home folder).

- **In Windows XP**—Open Windows Explorer and drag the downloaded file to this folder: MyDocuments/MyMusic/iTunes/ iTunes Plug-Ins.

- **In Windows Vista or Windows 7**—Open Windows Explorer and drag the downloaded file to this folder: Users/*yourname*/AppData/Roaming/Apple Computer/iTunes/ iTunes Plug-Ins (where *yourname* is your user name on the computer).

If you haven't yet installed any iTunes plug-ins, you'll need to create a subfolder inside your iTunes folder. Name it iTunes Plug-Ins so that iTunes can find it.

After you've installed a Visualizer plug-in, you'll find it on the fly-out menu that appears when you select View, Visualizer. You can select your new visualizer from there. Happy viewing!

Each third-party visualizer plug-in has its own set of commands, so those shown in Table 4.1 may not work with a new visualizer you've installed.

Whether you want mellow music or a danceable party mix, you can create a playlist that matches your mood. iTunes offers several kinds of playlists; this chapter covers them all.

5

Playing with Playlists

iTunes gives you several ways to gather songs together into playlists. You can pick and choose the tracks you want by hand, set up an ever-changing automatic mix, or have iTunes find songs that will go great together.

This chapter is all about playlists, from the basics of setting up a playlist and listening to its tunes, to using iTunes' cool automatic playlists: the iTunes DJ, which creates a live mix (and takes requests); smart playlists, which scour your music library to find songs that match criteria you set up; and Genius playlists and mixes, which look at the music you like and find other music that'll sound great with it.

Getting Started with Playlists

If you have music in your iTunes library, you already have some playlists—iTunes sets them up for you automatically. In the left source list, look under Playlists to see what's there. Automatically generated playlists are preceded by an icon that looks like a gear, as shown in Figure 5.1. You might find playlists organized by era (such as '90s music), genre, most played, top rated (if you rate your songs), recently purchased, and so on. Click any playlist to see its contents.

User-created playlists
Automatically generated playlists
Folder holding multiple playlists

Figure 5.1 *Playlists in iTunes*

SHOW ME   Media 5.1—Working with Playlists
Access this video file through your registered Web Edition at
my.safaribooksonline.com/9780132660273/media.

LET ME TRY IT

Creating a Playlist

Creating a new playlist in iTunes takes only a few steps:

1. In the lower-left corner of the iTunes window, click the Create a Playlist
    button (it looks like a plus sign—see Figure 5.2).

You can create a new playlist in two other ways: Press Ctrl+N (on a PC) or Cmd-N
(on a Mac), or go the menu route by selecting File, New Playlist.

2. A text box appears at the bottom of your existing playlists. Type the name of your new playlist in it.

3. Press Enter or click outside the text box to save the playlist's name.

4. To add songs to your playlist, click Music in your iTunes library. Select the songs you want and drag them onto your playlist.

You can drag songs one at a time or in groups (hold down the Shift key or the Ctrl/Cmd key as you select multiple songs). You can even add an entire album to your playlist—simply click and drag the cover art, and then drop it onto the playlist. The album's songs appear, in order, on the playlist.

When you buy music in the iTunes Store, iTunes automatically adds them to a playlist that records all your purchases. To see what's on it, look in the source list under Store and click Purchased.

Type playlist name here.
Click to create a new playlist.

Figure 5.2   *Creating a new playlist*

 Your playlist displays songs in the order in which you add them, but you can rearrange them in any order you like. **See** "Configuring a Playlist," coming up in this chapter.

You can rename an existing playlist at any time. Click the playlist's name, and it turns into a text box. Type the new name there. When you're done, press Enter or click outside the text box.

Opening a Playlist in a New Window

You might find it easier to drag songs from one window to another than to drag them across the iTunes window. That way, you can keep an eye on your playlist as you build it. To open a playlist in a new window, double-click the icon to the left of the playlist's name. When the playlist opens in a new window, you can see all its current tracks. Now you can browse your music library in the original window and drag new selections into the separate playlist window.

Selecting Songs First

You can also create a playlist by selecting songs first and then making a playlist to hold them. To do that, choose the songs you want and select File, New Playlist from Selection. Name the playlist; you can play it now or continue to add songs.

Playlists aren't restricted to just songs. You can put whatever's in your iTunes library in a playlist: audiobooks, podcasts, music videos, TV shows, and even movies. You can mix and match, too, combining songs and music videos, throwing in a TV episode—anything you want. If your iPod doesn't play video, however, it'll skip any videos on your playlist and play only audio files.

Adding a Song to an Existing Playlist

Dragging and dropping is one way to get songs into a playlist you've created, but there's another method—and it's quicker when you've built up a lot of playlists. When you come across a song you want to add to an existing playlist, select the song and right-click it. From the context menu, choose Add to Playlist. A submenu flies out, listing all your playlists. Click the one you want, and iTunes adds the selected song to the end of that playlist.

Using Playlists

Playlists are a great way to organize your iTunes library to focus on the music you want. When you have some playlists in iTunes, you can work with them in various ways—listen to a playlist, sort and edit its tracks, print it for a CD jewel case cover or to share with others, and organize related playlists into folders.

Listening to a Playlist

As Figure 5.1 shows, iTunes adds the playlists you create to the Playlists section of the left source list. To listen to a playlist, find the one you want in the source list and select it. When you select a playlist, its tracks appear in the main part of the iTunes window. You can start at the beginning or with any song you want. Double-click the song you want to hear, or select it and click the Play button.

When you sync iTunes with your portable device, your playlists sync, too. Or you can drag a playlist from iTunes to your device when your iPod, iPhone, or iPad is connected to your computer's USB port. Click the playlist you want, drag it to Devices in the source list, and drop it there to sync just that playlist.

Configuring a Playlist

Playlists aren't set in stone. You can sort them, rearrange tracks, or delete songs you don't want there. Read on to see just how flexible a playlist can be.

Sorting a Playlist

As with any list of tracks in iTunes, you can sort a playlist—by song title, length, artist, genre, and so on. Just click the header at the top of any column to sort by that column. If you want to reverse the sort order, click the header again.

To return to the original, unsorted order, click the header of the leftmost column (there's no column name in it).

 **LET ME TRY IT**

Saving a Sort

If you like the way you've sorted a playlist and want to save the tracks in their new, sorted order, you can. After you've sorted the playlist (keeping it open), do this:

1. In the iTunes source list, right-click the playlist.

2. In the context menu that opens, select Copy to Play Order.

iTunes makes the sorted order the new order for that playlist. Click the header of the far-left column to unsort the list; the order remains as it is.

Want to see which playlists a particular song appears in? Select the song and right-click (on a PC) or Ctrl-click (on a Mac). The context menu that pops up has an option called Show in Playlist. Point to that option, and a flyout menu lists the playlists in which the song appears. Click any playlist to open it with that song selected.

Changing Tracks' Order in a Playlist

You can create a playlist by adding tracks in any order. Whenever you want, you can rearrange the tracks to get just the right mix of tempos and styles. To move a track, select it and drag it up or down the list. As you drag, a horizontal black line follows (see Figure 5.3), indicating the track's new position. When you get the track where you want it, let go of the mouse button; the track drops into place beneath the horizontal line.

Figure 5.3 *Rearranging tracks in a playlist*

You can't change the order of tracks in a sorted playlist. Before you move tracks around on the list, make sure the playlist is in its original, unsorted order by clicking the header of the far-left column.

You can select multiple tracks to move them en masse. When you're dragging more than one track to a new position, iTunes indicates this by displaying a number that shows how many tracks you're moving. If you select and move nonadjacent tracks, iTunes places them next to each other when you drop them into their new location.

Deleting Tracks from a Playlist

Hey, how did that piano concerto get into your dance music playlist? When you want to remove a song from your playlist, right-click (on a PC) or Ctrl-click (on a Mac) the song you want to take off the list, and then select Delete from the contextual menu. Or you can select the song and then click Edit, Delete (on a PC) or iTunes, Delete (on a Mac).

The first time you delete a song from a playlist, iTunes asks you to confirm that you really want to remove the song. (If you don't want to see this message every single time you delete a song, click the Do Not Ask Me Again check box.) Click Remove to confirm the deletion.

Deleting a song from a playlist does not remove that song from your iTunes library.

Printing a Playlist

If you plan to burn your playlist to an audio CD, you can print the playlist in a format that fits a CD jewel case, creating a nice-looking cover for the CD. You have lots of options—for example, include cover art or not, print in color or black-and-white—for printing the list. You can also print your playlist's tracks as a simple list, which can be useful if you're going over the music for a party or other event with someone else.

G *See "Burning a CD or DVD" (in Chapter 8, "Managing Your iTunes Library") to find out how to create a CD from music in your iTunes library.*

To print a playlist, select the playlist you want to print and then choose File, Print. The Print dialog box, shown in Figure 5.4, opens. Choose one of these options from the Theme drop-down list:

- **CD Jewel Case Insert**—Choose this when you want to print an insert that will create a cover for an audio CD of your playlist. When you do, iTunes asks you to pick one of these printing options:

  - **Text Only**—Prints the track list (song titles and times, in order) on a colored background.

  - **Mosaic**—Prints the track list and a mosaic drawn from the cover artwork of the albums whose songs appear in the playlist. This option also uses a colored background.

  - **White Mosaic**—Is just like the mosaic option, except that the background is white. (The album covers in the mosaic are in color.)

  - **Single Cover**—Prints (in color) the album cover for the currently selected song, along with the track list.

  - **Text Only (Black & White)**—Prints the track list, with no art, in black and white.

  - **Mosaic (Black & White)**—Is just like the mosaic option, except that it prints in black and white, not color.

  - **Single Side (Black & White)**—Prints just the track list, leaving the other side blank. (This is great if you want to draw your own artwork.)

  - **Large Playlist (Black & White)**—Starts printing the track list on the front cover and continues onto the back cover. (This is great for a long playlist.)

- **Song Listing**—This prints a full-sheet version of your playlist that includes the name of the playlist and the title, length, artist, and album for each song. It's a good choice when you want to share your playlist with others.

- **Album Listing**—This prints your playlist on a full sheet so that it looks like Album List view, organizing the tracks on the playlist by album and including cover art (in color).

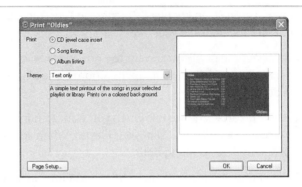

Figure 5.4   *Printing a playlist*

When you select a printing option, a preview window on the right side of the dialog box shows how the printed playlist will look. When you've selected the theme you want, click OK to print the playlist.

To change the orientation of how your playlist prints on the page, click the Page Setup button on the Print dialog box; then select Portrait or Landscape, as you prefer, and click OK. The Page Setup dialog box also lets you adjust the margins or change the paper size.

Organizing Playlists into Folders

If you're a fanatic for a certain kind of music, you'll end up creating a number of different yet related playlists. With time, it can be hard to find the playlist you're looking for as you scroll down a long list of options. Clean up your source list and organize your playlists by creating folders and then storing related playlists in a relevant folder.

 LET ME TRY IT

Creating a Playlist Folder

Here's how to create a folder that holds related playlists:

1. In iTunes, select File, New Playlist Folder. iTunes inserts the folder in the Playlists section of the source list.

2. Type a name for the folder that describes the kind of playlists the folder will hold.

3. Press Enter or click outside the text box where you typed the folder's name.

4. Drag playlists into the folder to store them there.

> If you're creating a brand-new playlist that you want to store in a folder, select the folder and then click the Create New Playlist button. iTunes adds the new playlist to the selected folder. You can drag playlists from one folder to another. You can also nest subfolders inside a folder.

The iTunes DJ

There's a DJ in your computer that can create live mixes of your songs, take requests, and continually update the evolving playlist. The iTunes DJ does all this, setting up live mixes of music drawn from your library or a playlist. After one song has played, the DJ adds a new track to the end of the playlist, so the music mix keeps going until the party's over.

SHOW ME   Media 5.2—Using the iTunes DJ
Access this video file through your registered Web Edition at
my.safaribooksonline.com/9780132660273/media.

LET ME TRY IT

Creating an iTunes DJ Live Mix

Getting the iTunes DJ up and running takes only a few steps:

1. In the Playlists section of the iTunes navigation bar, click iTunes DJ.

2a. The first time you start the DJ, iTunes shows you an info page. Click Continue. iTunes displays a playlist of 15 randomly selected songs.

2b. Select the source for the songs the DJ will mix: From the lower-left Source drop-down list, select Music (which pulls songs from your entire Music library) or choose the playlist you want for the mix.

3. Click the lower-right Settings button to open the iTunes DJ Settings dialog box, shown in Figure 5.5.

4a. Tell iTunes how many songs you want to see in the playlist (both previously played and upcoming).

4b. If you rate your iTunes songs and want to hear your favorites more often than the rest, click to put a check mark in the box labeled Play Higher Rated Songs More Often.

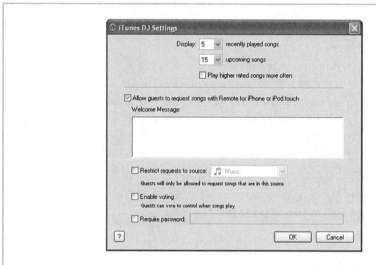

Figure 5.5   *iTunes DJ settings*

4c. Click OK to apply these settings.

5. Click Play to start playing the DJ mix.

🅖 *The iTunes DJ Settings dialog box (see Figure 5.5) is also where you set up the Remote app for use with the iTunes DJ.* **See** *"Letting Guests Request Songs," coming up in this chapter.*

Editing an iTunes DJ Playlist

Unlike its more intelligent counterparts—the Smart and Genius playlists—the iTunes DJ just grabs songs from your library at random and lines them up to play. Fortunately, you can tweak DJ playlists to make sure the DJ is playing what you want to hear. You can edit the iTunes DJ playlist in these ways:

- **To change all the songs in the iTunes DJ playlist**—Click the lower-right Refresh button.

- **To change the order of songs in the iTunes DJ playlist**—Select a track you want to move, drag it to its new location, and drop it there—just as you would with any of your iTunes playlists.

- **To add a song to the iTunes DJ playlist**—Use the same drag-and-drop method: Find the song in your library and drag it into the iTunes DJ playlist.

- **To remove a song from the iTunes DJ playlist**—Right-click the song and select Delete from the context menu. If you're prompted to confirm the deletion, click Remove. iTunes removes the selected song from your playlist and replaces it with another track.

Letting Guests Request Songs

Just like a real, live DJ, the iTunes DJ takes requests. When you're playing your iTunes DJ music mix at a party, guests can use an iPhone, iPod Touch, or iPad to request a song using the Remote app (the next section shows how). Before they can do that, however, you have to set up the iTunes DJ to take requests.

 LET ME TRY IT

Setting Up the iTunes DJ to Take Requests

To allow your iTunes DJ to take requests, follow these steps:

1. Under Playlists, click iTunes DJ.

2. Click the lower-right Settings button.

3. In the iTunes DJ Settings dialog box (refer to Figure 5.5), click to put a check mark in the box labeled Allow Guests to Request Songs with Remote for iPhone or iPod Touch.

4a. Type an optional message into the Welcome Message box. This customizes the message your guests see when they use Remote to request a song.

4b. If you don't want guests rummaging through your entire Music library, select the Restrict Requests to Source check box and choose the playlist you want guests to use.

4c. If you want guests to be able to pick which song plays next, check the Enable Voting check box.

4d. You can require a password so that only guests who have that password can request or vote on a song. (This can be useful if you want to change the playlist from your iPhone but you don't want anyone else tinkering with your playlist.) Select the Require Password check box and type in a password for iTunes to recognize.

5. Click OK.

You've set up the Remote app to work with your iTunes DJ. The next section tells how to use that app.

 LET ME TRY IT

Requesting a Song Remotely

After you've enabled requests, you (or your guests) can browse your iTunes library from an iPod Touch, iPhone, or iPad and request any song. To do that, download Apple's Remote app from the App Store to your portable device. When it's installed, here's how to tell the iTunes DJ what to play:

1. Tap the Remote app to open it. You'll see a page similar to the one shown in Figure 5.6.

2. The iTunes DJ section lists the library the DJ is using. Tap that library to open it.

3a. If the iTunes DJ playlist is protected, type in its password and tap Return.

3b. The iTunes DJ playlist appears, as shown in Figure 5.7, with the current song at the top. Tap Request a Song.

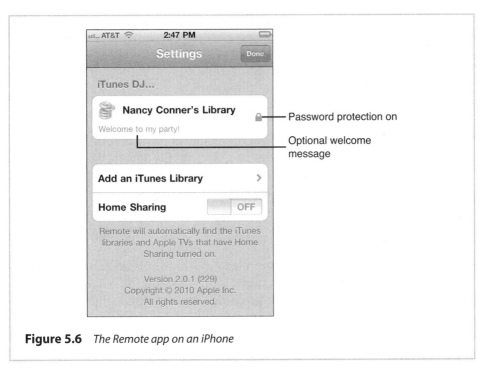

Figure 5.6 *The Remote app on an iPhone*

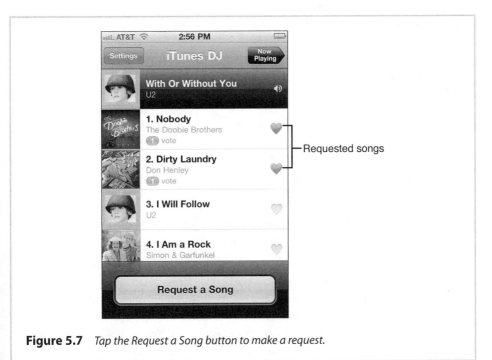

Figure 5.7 *Tap the Request a Song button to make a request.*

4. Your screen shows a list of available artists. Tap any artist to see that artist's songs.

5. Tap a song to request it. The iTunes DJ adds it to the playlist.

Hiding the iTunes DJ Playlist

If you don't want the iTunes DJ showing in your list of playlists, select Edit, Preferences (on a PC) or iTunes, Preferences (on a Mac). On the General tab, remove the check mark from the iTunes DJ check box and click OK. The iTunes DJ disappears from the Playlists section of the navigation bar.

Smart Playlists

In iTunes, a smart playlist plays by the rules—your rules. You tell iTunes the kinds of songs you want to put together into a playlist. iTunes scours your library to find the tracks that match your criteria and then gathers those tracks together into a playlist. That's smart.

 SHOW ME   Media 5.3—Creating a Smart Playlist
Access this video file through your registered Web Edition at
my.safaribooksonline.com/9780132660273/media.

 **LET ME TRY IT**

Creating a Smart Playlist

Here's how to set up the rules to create a smart playlist:

1. In your iTunes library, select File, New Smart Playlist (or press Ctrl/Cmd+Alt+N).

2. In the Smart Playlist dialog box (see Figure 5.8), make sure the Match the Following Rule check box is selected.

3a. Tell iTunes what to play. Create your rule by choosing from the drop-down lists. You can limit selections to a particular genre, artist, and year (and those are just a few of your many choices), and tell iTunes to add only songs that meet a particular criterion that you define. For example, you could set up a rule like "Genre is not Classical" or "Year is 1994." You could even choose a theme with a rule like "Name contains love."

To narrow your playlist further, you can add more rules. Click the plus sign (+) to the right of a rule to add a new one. To add a new set of rules, click the ellipsis (...) button. When you have more than one rule defining your smart playlist, be sure to tell iTunes whether to match *all* rules you've defined or *any* of them.

3b. Tell iTunes how to add songs to the playlist. Specify how big the playlist will be (by number of items, length, or file size), and then tell iTunes how to select items: randomly, by artist or album, or by rating or play frequency (those are just some of your options).

3c. If you want to skip some items that satisfy the rule, select the Match Only Checked Items box (and make sure the items you want excluded *don't* have a check mark to the left of the track name).

3d. To automatically update your smart playlist with new items that you add to your iTunes library, make sure the Live Updating box is checked. When live updating is on, iTunes checks new additions to your library to see whether they match the playlist's rules and adds those that qualify to the playlist.

4. Click OK to create your playlist.

Figure 5.8   *Creating a new smart playlist*

The real power of smart playlists comes from your ability to set up multiple rules to specify exactly what you want. Figure 5.9 shows an example of a smart playlist that uses several rules, creating a playlist that includes songs from the Rock/Pop playlist with a rating of five stars that haven't been played in the past week. You could hunt through your iTunes library to create such a playlist yourself, but a smart playlist does a more thorough (and faster) job.

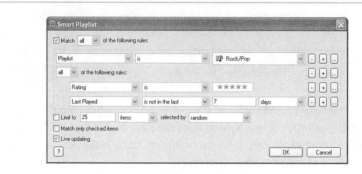

Figure 5.9 *Creating a smart playlist with multiple rules*

Editing a Smart Playlist

You can tweak what's on a smart playlist by changing its rules. To do that, select the smart playlist you want to edit and choose File, Edit Smart Playlist. This opens the Smart Playlist dialog box (similar to the one shown in Figure 5.9, but with the current rules displayed). You can change an existing rule by changing its criteria (choose a different item from a drop-down list or revise what's in the text box). You can also edit a smart playlist in these ways:

- **Add a new rule**—Click the plus sign (+) to the right of any existing rule to add another criterion.

- **Add a new set of rules**—Want to get more specific? Click the ellipsis (...) to add a whole new set of subrules to a rule in the playlist.

- **Delete a rule**—To remove a rule from your playlist's selection criteria, click the minus sign (-) to its right.

- **Change the number of items on the playlist**—Select the Limit To box and tell iTunes how to limit the size of the playlist.

- **Keep a particular song off the playlist**—This is a two-step operation. First, find the song you don't want on the playlist and remove the check mark to the left of its title. Then, in the Smart Playlist dialog box, select the Match Only Checked Items box. The unchecked song won't appear on the playlist.

To delete a smart playlist, right-click it in the source list and then select Delete from the context menu.

Better Than Smart: Genius Playlists

Beginning with iTunes 9, iTunes introduced its smartest playlist yet—so smart, they called it Genius. Whereas smart playlists use your criteria to create playlists, Genius playlists go a step further. Genius analyzes your iTunes library, as well as those of other Genius users with similar tastes, and creates great mixes of your existing music—and also recommends music that you might like but don't currently have in your library.

TELL ME MORE   Media 5.4—Genius, Your Information, and Privacy

Access this audio recording through your registered Web Edition at
my.safaribooksonline.com/9780132660273/media.

Turning on Genius means sharing information about your iTunes library with Apple. That enables Apple to use that information to make informed choices for your Genius mixes and recommendations for other music you might like.

Here's how it works: When you turn on Genius, iTunes periodically sends information about your iTunes library, such as track names, ratings, and how many times you've played songs. This info is combined with your iTunes Store purchase history and kept under an anonymous Genius ID, which is not linked to your iTunes account. Apple then combines your anonymous info with the anonymous info of other Genius users to get the best recommendations. You'll benefit from information provided by other iTunes users who share your tastes in music to discover new songs and interesting mixes.

Getting Started with Genius

Before you can put iTunes' resident Genius to work for you, you need to turn it on. To do that, click Genius in the left navigation bar (or select Store, Turn On Genius) to open the page shown in Figure 5.10, which spells out the benefits of using Genius. Click the lower-right Turn On Genius button.

Sign in to your iTunes Store account (or, if you haven't set one up yet, select Create a New iTunes Store Account). Click Continue. Read the Terms of Service and click to put a check mark in the box to indicate that you agree. Click Continue.

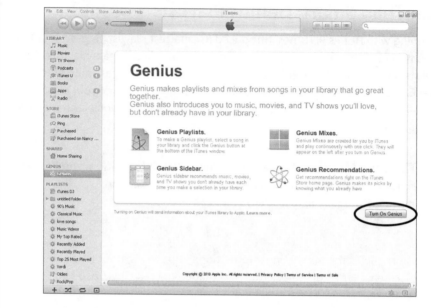

Figure 5.10   *Turning on Genius*

Genius goes to work. It takes a few minutes for Genius to get up and running. During this time, here's what Genius is doing:

- Gathering information about your iTunes library

- Sending that information to Apple

- Sending your Genius results back to you

While this process takes place, you can continue to use iTunes as you normally would. When you see Genius Mixes appear under Genius in the navigation bar, Genius is ready for you to use.

Listening to a Genius Mix

After you've set up Genius, iTunes automatically creates a Genius Mix for your listening pleasure. A Genius Mix selects songs from your iTunes library and plays them continuously. It's kind of like listening to a commercial-free radio station stocked with all your favorite music. Genius even sets up different mixes for different kinds of music in your library.

Genius Mixes appear under Genius in the left source list. To listen to one, click Genius Mixes. Find the mix you want and double-click it to listen.

Creating a Genius Playlist

Creating a Genius playlist is a snap—just select any song in your iTunes library and click the lower-right Genius button. Genius immediately creates a playlist of songs based on your selection.

From there, you can:

- **Listen to the Genius playlist**—Just click Play to hear the selected song and listen to the other tunes in the playlist.

- **Change the number of songs on the list**—The default number of songs for a Genius playlist is 25, but you can keep the party going with 50, 75, or even 100 songs by making a selection from the upper-right Limit To dropdown list.

- **Refresh the playlist**—Not quite what you were looking for? Even Genius can make a mistake. Click the upper-right Refresh button for a different mix (it's still based on the song you selected).

- **Save the playlist**—If you love the mix that Genius came up with, click the upper-right Save Playlist button. iTunes saves the playlist and adds it to the navigation bar under Genius, using the name of the first song as the playlist's name. To rename the playlist, click its name; when the name changes to a text box, type in its new name.

Getting Genius Recommendations

When you're shopping in a physical store, flesh-and-blood salespeople are ready to listen to your preferences and help you with recommendations. In the iTunes Store, Genius does the same thing (minus any hard-sell pressure). Genius already knows what music you've bought, and it uses that information—along with information from other shoppers with similar tastes—to recommend music you might enjoy.

On the home page of the iTunes Store, go to the Quick Links list on the right and select Genius Recommendations. You'll see a page like the one in Figure 5.11. Genius explains why it's made each suggestion—you bought music by guitar wizard Eric Clapton, for example, so you might like the guitar artistry of Santana, too. Or you have an album of opera arias that you transferred to your Music library from a CD, so Genius suggests other operas you might want to try.

Choose a genre from the upper-right Genre drop-down list to target a specific kind of music in your library.

To help Genius fine-tune its recommendations, you can give its suggestions a thumbs-up or a thumbs-down (just click the appropriate icon by any suggestion). After you've rated a suggestion—whether you like it or not—that suggestion no longer appears among your Genius Recommendations.

Genius recommendations aren't limited to music. You can also get recommendations for movies and TV shows, based on your Genius information. Scroll down the Genius Recommendations page to see what Genius is suggesting for all your favorite forms of entertainment.

Figure 5.11 *Getting Genius recommendations in the iTunes Store*

Updating Your Genius Information

Genius normally updates your information once a week, when you're online and signed into iTunes. If you just added a great new album to your iTunes library and you want Genius to take it into account for mixes and recommendations, you can tell Genius to do an update right now.

To update your Genius information manually, select Store, Update Genius. iTunes sends your information to Apple, which returns new Genius results and updates your mixes.

Turning Off Genius

If you've given Genius a try and decided it isn't for you, you can turn it off. When you turn off Genius, iTunes no longer sends information about your library to Apple. Your Genius Mixes disappear, and any Genius playlists get converted to ordinary playlists. You can't create a new Genius playlist unless you turn Genius back on.

To stop using Genius, select Store, Turn Off Genius. A dialog box asks whether you're sure you want to do this. Click the Turn Off Genius button. iTunes turns off Genius; you can find any saved playlists you created using Genius in the Playlists section of the source list.

If you miss Genius and want it back, you can simply turn it on again. Follow the instructions in "Getting Started with Genius," earlier in this chapter.

iTunes is about way more than music. You can also watch your favorite videos—on your computer, your iPod, or your TV (via Apple TV). So click Play and enjoy!

6

Viewing in iTunes: TV, Movies, and More

iTunes puts a whole world of video entertainment right at your fingertips. You can buy—or rent—movies and TV shows right from the iTunes Store. This chapter shows you how to use iTunes as your very own on-demand movie theater. Watch videos in iTunes and choose playback settings for the best viewing experience. You'll also learn about using Apple TV, a device that lets you stream content from your iTunes library to your widescreen TV. The chapter ends with a quick discussion of iTunes and iBooks, the ebooks you can read on your iPod Touch, iPhone, or iPad.

Watching Videos in iTunes

iTunes includes a built-in video player that lets you watch videos of many different types:

- Movies
- TV shows
- Music videos
- Video podcasts
- Video courses from iTunes U

Each kind of video is stored in the relevant section of your iTunes library. If you want to watch a movie, for example, click Movies to find the one you want. If you rent a video from the iTunes Store, iTunes puts it in the Rentals section until the rental period expires.

To learn how to rent videos from the iTunes Store, **see** "Renting Movies and TV Shows" (in Chapter 3, "Shopping in the iTunes Store"). For more on watching rentals, **see** "Watching Rented Videos" (coming up in this chapter).

Whatever kind of video you're watching in iTunes, the process is the same: Select the video you want to watch and take one of these actions:

- Double-click the video.

- Click Play in the Controls bar.

The video player launches, and your video starts immediately, as shown in Figure 6.1. Depending on your playback settings, the video shows in the iTunes window (see Figure 6.1), a separate window, the lower-left artwork viewer, or full-screen.

You can tell iTunes how you want to launch a video when you play it. **See** "Selecting Video Playback Settings" (later in this chapter).

The video continues to play until either it reaches the end or you stop it. (Click Pause to stop playback.) When you stop a video, iTunes remembers your place. Even if you close iTunes and come back later, when you play the video again, it starts where you left off.

Figure 6.1   *Playing a video in the iTunes window*

What about watching a DVD that you insert in your computer's CD/DVD drive? You can listen to CDs through iTunes, but you can't use iTunes to watch a DVD this way. Movies and other videos must be in your iTunes library for you to view them.

 SHOW ME   Media 6.1—Watching a Video in iTunes
Access this video file through your registered Web Edition at ***my.safaribooksonline.com/9780132660273/media.***

Using Playback Controls

When you hover your mouse pointer over a video, its playback controls appear (you can see these in Figure 6.1). Figure 6.2 shows what you can control as a video plays:

- **Volume**—Move the slider to the right to increase volume or left to decrease it.

- **Watch the Previous Video**—This button plays the previous video in your library.

- **Rewind**—Well, "rewind" is what they *used* to call it in the days of videotapes and VCRs. Click and hold this button to scan backward through the video.

- **Play/Pause**—When the video is playing, click this button to pause the action. Click it again to resume playback.

- **Fast Forward**—Click and hold this button to scan forward in the video.

- **Watch the Next Video**—Maybe you realize you've already seen this episode of a TV show. Click this button to move to the next video in your library.

- **Select a Scene**—Movies consist of multiple scenes, organized into chapters. You can select and move to a different chapter using the Scene menu.

- **Subtitles**—Click this button to toggle subtitles on or off.

Ⓖ *To set up subtitles to work with your iTunes videos,* **see** *"Turning on Subtitles" (coming up in this chapter).*

- **Full Screen**—Clicking this button is a quick way to switch to full-screen viewing. In full-screen mode, click again to shrink the player.

Toggle back and forth between full-screen and standard view by pressing Ctrl+F
(on a PC) or Cmd-F (on a Mac).

Beneath the playback control buttons is a slider. At the slider's left end, a counter
tells you how much of the video has played; the counter on the right shows you
how much time is left in the video. Drag the slider left to scan backward in the
video or right to scan forward.

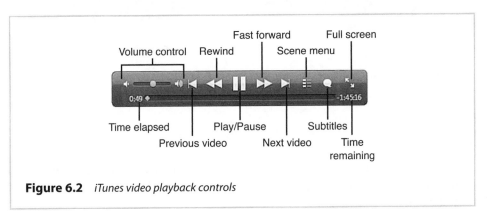

Figure 6.2   *iTunes video playback controls*

Jumping to a Different Scene

Long videos, such as movies, are divided into scenes, just as a book is divided into
chapters. Breaking a movie into scenes helps you navigate through a long video,
making it easy to find your favorite parts.

To jump to a different part of a video as it plays, move the mouse pointer to show
the playback controls. Click the Scene Menu button (see Figure 6.2). A menu
appears, like the example in Figure 6.3, showing the movie's different scenes. Each
scene has a title and a picture that shows the start of that scene. Click the scene
you want to play.

Figure 6.3   *Select a scene to jump to it.*

Turning On Subtitles

If you're watching a video in a language that you don't speak, subtitles let you follow the action by translating what's being said—the words appear at the bottom of the screen.

To use subtitles, first you have to turn them on. Select Edit, Preferences (on a PC) or iTunes, Preferences (on a Mac), and click the Playback tab. From the Subtitle language drop-down list, choose the language you want and then click OK. When a movie is playing that has subtitles available, the Subtitles button appears in the playback controls (see Figure 6.2). Click that button to turn subtitles on or off.

Using Closed Captioning in Videos

Closed captioning displays a transcript of a program's audio so that people with a hearing disability can follow what's being said by reading the transcript. To turn on closed captioning, select Edit, Preferences (on a PC) or iTunes, Preferences (on a Mac); click the Playback tab; and click to put a check mark in the box labeled Show Closed Captioning When Available. Then click OK. Not all videos come with closed captioning, but those that do automatically display captions when you turn on this setting.

To find closed-captioned movies in the iTunes Store, use Power Search. On the iTunes Store's home page, click the Power Search Quick Link. Select Movies from the left drop-down list. When the search fields change to reflect criteria for movies, click to put a check mark in the Search Only for Movies That Contain Closed Captioning check box. Now when you do your search, results are limited to closed-captioned movies.

Watching Rented Videos

You can rent both movies and TV shows through the iTunes Store. When you rent a video, you have 30 days to watch it. (If you don't, the rental expires and the video disappears from your iTunes library.) When you've started watching a video, you have 24 hours to watch the whole thing. (That's if you're in the U.S. Residents of other countries may have up to 48 hours to watch it.) At the end of that time, the video is removed from your library.

 To read about renting movies and TV shows through the iTunes Store, **see** "Renting Movies and TV Shows" (in Chapter 3).

When you have an active rental (one that's available for you to watch), you'll find it in the Rentals section of your iTunes library, shown in Figure 6.4. This section appears only when you've rented a movie or TV show, so you won't always see it in the source list. When you click Rentals, iTunes shows you your available rentals and lets you know how long you have left to watch them before they expire. As with any video, double-click a rental (or select it and click Play) to watch it.

 SHOW ME   Media 6.2—Renting and Watching Videos in iTunes
Access this video file through your registered Web Edition at
my.safaribooksonline.com/9780132660273/media.

When the rental clock ticks down from days to hours, iTunes lets you know that your rental has almost expired. When you open iTunes, you'll see a dialog box letting you know that the rental period is about to end. (If you don't want this reminder, select the box labeled Do Not Warn Me About Expiring Rentals.) Click OK to close the box.

In addition, when there's a nearly expired rental in your iTunes library, the source list's Rentals icon (which looks like a movie ticket) turns red. The remaining time to watch also appears in red when a rental is about to expire (see Figure 6.4).

Figure 6.4   *iTunes lets you know when video rentals will expire.*

Selecting Video Playback Settings

If you find yourself launching a video in the iTunes window and then immediately switching to full screen, you'll be glad to know that you can set iTunes to play back video the way you want to see it.

 LET ME TRY IT

Choosing Playback Settings

iTunes gives you choices about how you watch your movies and other videos. To set your playback preferences, follow these steps:

1. Select Edit, Preferences (on a PC) or iTunes, Preferences (on a Mac).

2. Click the Playback tab, shown in Figure 6.5.

3a. Choose one of these options from the Play Movies and TV Shows drop-down list:

    In the Artwork Viewer—Not exactly a big-screen experience, this option plays your video in the small pane in the lower-left part of the screen that usually displays cover art.

If you're watching a video in the artwork viewer, click the video as it's playing to open it in its own window.

In the iTunes Window—This option opens a large video viewer inside the iTunes window, as shown earlier in Figure 6.1, so you still see the controls bar at the top of the window and the status bar at the bottom. Click the upper-right *x* to stop playing the video.

In a Separate Window—This option opens the video player in its own window, which you can resize. Figure 6.6 shows an example. If you're not hiding the lower-left artwork viewer, the artwork for the item you're watching (such as the DVD cover) also appears there. If you want to do other things in iTunes as your video plays, this is a good choice.

To adjust the size of the video player window, click and drag the window's lower-right corner until it's the size you want.

Full Screen—When you want to give your full attention to the video you're watching, this is a good choice.

Full Screen (with Visuals)—If you create playlists that mix videos and music, choosing this option shows both videos full screen and, for the music tracks, full-screen visuals. This is a fun choice for a party playlist that combines music videos with audio tracks.

ⓖ *To read about adding visual effects to your music tracks,* **see** *"Watching Your Music with the iTunes Visualizer" (in Chapter 4, "Listening in iTunes").*

3b. Select an option for how you want to watch music videos from the Play Music Videos drop-down list. Your choices are the same as for other kinds of videos (listed in step 3a).

3c. If you don't want the default (English), make a selection from the Audio Language drop-down list. If a movie offers soundtracks in different languages (such as a movie whose dialogue is also dubbed into Spanish or French), iTunes will play the audio in the language you chose.

3d. By default, subtitles are turned off. If you want to see them, choose your language from the Subtitle Language drop-down list.

3e. The iTunes Store offers both standard-definition and high-definition videos. Videos shown in high definition are sharper, but playback may be spotty on an older or slower computer. If you have problems viewing your videos in iTunes, try selecting the box labeled Play Videos Using Standard Definition Version.

ⓖ *To decide whether to watch videos in high or standard definition, listen to "Standard Definition or HD?" (Media 6.4).*

3f. Closed captioning, explained earlier in this chapter, is available for many movies and TV shows. If you want to see the transcript as the show plays, put a check mark in the box labeled Show Closed Captioning When Available.

4. When you get all your video playback preferences set the way you want them, click OK to apply your settings.

Figure 6.5 *Setting playback preferences for video*

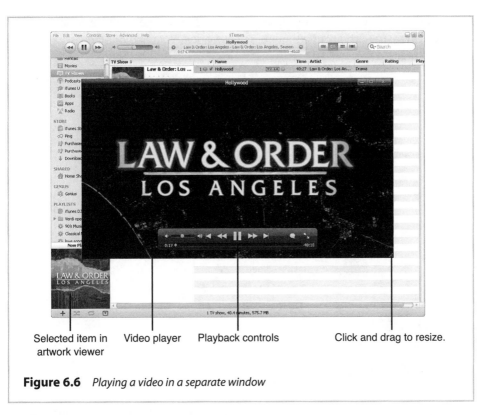

Selected item in   Video player   Playback controls   Click and drag to resize.
artwork viewer

Figure 6.6 *Playing a video in a separate window*

 SHOW ME   Media 6.3—Playing a Mixed Video/Music Playlist
Access this video file through your registered Web Edition at
my.safaribooksonline.com/9780132660273/media.

 TELL ME MORE   Media 6.4—Standard Definition or HD?
Access this audio recording through your registered Web Edition at
my.safaribooksonline.com/9780132660273/media.

Marking a Video Viewed or Not Viewed

When you look at your list of videos in a section of your iTunes library (Movies or TV Shows, for example), iTunes shows an icon that gives the status of each one, as shown in Figure 6.7. The icon appears to the left of the video's title and indicates whether it's downloading, unwatched, or partially watched. No icon means that you've watched that video.

You can change a video's status from unwatched to watched, or vice versa. Right-click a video; from the context menu, select Mark as Watched or Mark as Unwatched.

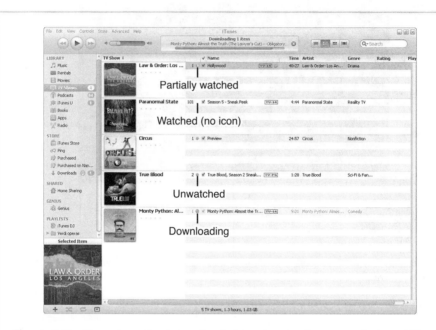

Figure 6.7   *iTunes shows the status of each video: downloading, unwatched, partially watched, or watched.*

Apple TV and iTunes

Apple TV is a digital media receiver that works with iTunes and your widescreen television set or home theater. You can use it to stream the videos in your iTunes library (music, too) directly to your TV, enhancing your viewing experience.

Here's a sampling of what you can do with Apple TV:

- Stream movies, TV shows, music, and photos to your home theater.

- Rent movies and TV shows directly from the iTunes Store. No discs to return—ever.

- Stream movies directly from Netflix for on-demand viewing.

- Watch YouTube videos on your TV.

This section focuses on making iTunes and Apple TV work together. It covers the newest, second-generation version of Apple TV (easier to use than ever) and, for first-generation users, gives the basics of using that version of Apple TV with iTunes.

Streaming Your iTunes Library to Apple TV

Through Home Sharing, your second-generation Apple TV has immediate, real-time access to your iTunes library, so you can find any movie or TV show in your library and watch it immediately on your TV. You can even listen to your iTunes music collection through your home theater. To make Apple TV work with iTunes, start by turning on Home Sharing for the computer that holds your iTunes library.

ⓒ *To find out how to turn on Home Sharing,* **see** *"Getting Started with Home Sharing" (in Chapter 9, "Syncing and Sharing").*

After you've turned on Home Sharing for that computer, you need to turn it on for your second-generation Apple TV. In Apple TV, select Settings, Computers; then select Turn On Home Sharing. Enter your Apple ID and password (use the same account you used to turn on Home Sharing for your computer). Apple TV activates Home Sharing, and now you have access to your iTunes library—right from your television set.

Formatting a Movie to Work with Apple TV

Some of the movies in your iTunes library may require conversion before you can watch them on your television through Apple TV. (This is also true for some movies that you may want to play on your iPod, iPhone, or iPad.) To convert a movie so that it plays on Apple TV, select the movie and then select Advanced, Create iPad or Apple TV Version.

iTunes starts the process of converting your movie—it can take anywhere from a few minutes to several hours to complete the conversion.

When you convert a movie to view using Apple TV or an iPad, the original file remains in your iTunes library.

Formatting Videos You've Made for Apple TV

Home movies—from a vacation or a family event, or just from fooling around with your friends—look great when you can watch them on a widescreen TV. If you've recorded videos and stored them in iTunes, you can play those on Apple TV. First, though, you have to make sure they're in a format that will play on Apple TV.

In iTunes, select the homemade video you want and then select Advanced, Create Apple TV Version. iTunes formats the video so that it will play in both iTunes and Apple TV.

Alternatively, you can use QuickTime Pro to convert a home movie to an Apple TV–compatible format. Open QuickTime Player and start the video. Select File, Export, Movie to Apple TV to save the file in a usable format.

If a video plays on your iPod, iPhone, or iPad, it will play on Apple TV.

Displaying Your Photos on Apple TV

If you want to share wedding photos, vacation pics, or new-baby pictures with family and friends, you can set up a slide show on your television set through Apple TV.

 LET ME TRY IT

Streaming Photos from Your Computer to Apple TV

It's easy to select photos that you've stored on your computer and stream them to your television set through Apple TV.

ⓖ *The directions that follow are for second-generation Apple TVs. To learn how to stream photos to a first-generation Apple TV, **see** "Streaming Photos from Your Computer to Your First-Generation Apple TV" (later in this chapter).*

To display your computer's photos via Apple TV, open iTunes and take these steps:

1. Select Advanced, Choose Photos to Share.

2. In the Photo Sharing Preferences dialog box (see Figure 6.8), put a check mark in the Share Photos From check box.

3. Choose a source for your photos: Select the folder on your computer that holds the photos you want to share.

4a. If you want to stream images from all subfolders in the source, choose All Folders.

4b. If you want to stream images from only certain subfolders in the source, choose Selected Folders and put a check mark beside the folder(s) you want.

5. Click Apply.

As you select folders, iTunes adds up how many photos are in the folders you've chosen and shows you the total in the upper-right corner of the Photo Sharing Preferences dialog box.

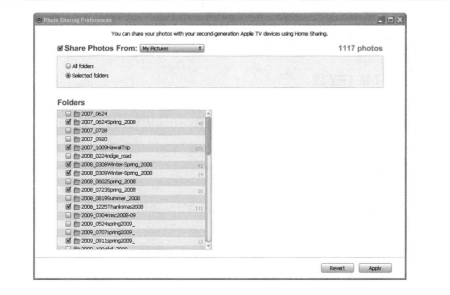

Figure 6.8 *Selecting photos to share*

First-Generation Apple TV

In September 2010, Apple released its second-generation Apple TV: a new, smaller, streamlined version of the device. But lots of people still use their first-generation Apple TV receiver. If that's you, your first-generation Apple TV works with iTunes 10, but you need to do things a bit differently from second-generation Apple TV folks. This section tells first-generation Apple TV owners how to stream their iTunes libraries, sync Apple TV with iTunes, and stream photos through Apple TV.

 LET ME TRY IT

Setting Up Your First-Generation Apple TV to Work with iTunes

Second-generation Apple TV users can stream videos from the iTunes library to Apple TV just by turning on Home Sharing. If your device is first-generation, you need to follow these steps to get set up:

1. Open iTunes.

2. In Apple TV, select Settings, Computers, Add Shared iTunes Library.

3. Apple TV shows you a passcode. Make a note of it—you'll need it back in iTunes.

4. In the iTunes source list, select Apple TV under Devices.

5. Type in the passcode you got from Apple TV.

 LET ME TRY IT

Syncing Your First-Generation Apple TV with iTunes

After you've set up your first-generation Apple TV to work with iTunes, you need to sync the device with your iTunes library. (Syncing isn't necessary for second-generation Apple TVs.) Here's how to get Apple TV in sync with iTunes:

1. In iTunes, select Edit, Preferences (on a PC) or iTunes, Preferences (on a Mac).

2. Select Apple TV and then select Look for Apple TVs.

3. In Apple TV, select Settings, Computers, Connect to iTunes.

4. Apple TV shows you a passcode. Make a note of it—you'll need it back in iTunes.

5. In iTunes, look under Devices in the source list and click Apple TV.

6. Type in the passcode you got from Apple TV.

7. Click Summary.

8a. If you want new items you add to iTunes to be added automatically to Apple TV, select Automatic Sync.

8b. If you prefer to choose which items sync between iTunes and Apple TV, select Custom Sync and then specify what you want to sync.

9. Click OK.

> When you sync iTunes and a first-generation Apple TV, the sync adds items to Apple TV in this order: movies, TV shows, music, podcasts, photos. (If your Apple TV runs out of space, the sync stops.)

Watching a Rented Movie with Your First-Generation Apple TV

After you've set up and synced your first-generation Apple TV with iTunes, you can use Apple TV to watch movies you've rented from the iTunes Store. To do this, you need to have iTunes open and your computer connected to the Internet. In iTunes, select Apple TV (under Devices) and click Videos. Choose the rental you want to watch, and click Move to transfer it.

 LET ME TRY IT

Streaming Photos from Your Computer to Your First-Generation Apple TV

To display a slideshow of photos from your computer on your first-generation Apple TV, follow these steps:

1. In iTunes, find Apple TV in the source list. (It's under Devices.) Select it.

2. Click the Photos button.

3. Select the photos you want for your slideshow.

4. Click Apply.

When you sync iTunes and a first-generation Apple TV, the sync adds photos last. If you want photos to sync first, select Sync Photos Before Other Media in the Photos pane.

iTunes and iBooks

With the advent of the iPad in 2010, Apple created iBooks, a free app for organizing and reading ebooks on your iPod Touch, iPhone, or iPad. iBooks-compatible books are in Apple's EPUB (short for "electronic publication") format, and you can also read PDFs (documents saved in Portable Document Format) using iBooks.

After you've downloaded iBooks to your device from Apple's App Store, you can find books in the iBookstore (access is included in the app) and read them on your device. Downloaded books appear in your iBooks library, as shown in Figure 6.9.

Figure 6.9 *An iBooks library on an iPhone. Tap the buttons at the top to switch between books and PDFs.*

If someone sends you an email with a PDF attached, you can open the document with iBooks and read it there. When you view a PDF email attachment, tap Open in iBooks. (You'll find it in the upper-right corner of your screen.) iBooks opens, displaying the PDF.

iTunes isn't an eBook reader; you can't use it to read the iBooks you get from the iBookstore. For years, though, iTunes has been able to recognize PDFs and open them with your computer's default PDF reader (such as Adobe Acrobat). This is how iTunes has handled the liner notes that come with some albums. (These booklets get stored in your Music library—you can identify a PDF by the book icon that appears to the right of its name.)

Click Books in the left iTunes source list to see what's in your iBooks library, as shown in Figure 6.10. As with a track list, you can sort the list or search for specific entries. The Books section lists both ebooks and audiobooks; an ebook shows a book icon to the right of its title; an audiobook lists its playing time (as with the selected item in Figure 6.10). Double-click an audiobook to play it in iTunes.

Figure 6.10   *Books listed in iTunes*

In iBooks, you can sample a book before you buy it by downloading a limited number of pages. Samples in your iBooks library don't appear in your list of books in iTunes.

As you add more content to your iTunes library, you'll want make sure you can always find the song, movie, or other content you want. This chapter shows you how to get—and stay—organized.

7

Organizing Your Content

You probably began filling up your iTunes library with a few favorite albums. Over time, you may have ripped your entire CD collection to add more content, shopped in the iTunes Store, and found other content by checking out your favorite artists' websites. And because iTunes lets you enjoy so many different kinds of content—music, videos, audiobooks, podcasts, and more—you probably diversified your collection as well. It seems that the more you use iTunes, the more crowded your iTunes library gets.

This chapter helps you organize the contents of your iTunes library so that you can find what you want when you want it. You'll read about how iTunes uses tags to find and organize media files—and how you can use those tags to make sure your library stays organized. You'll get the best strategies for organizing different kinds of content and learn how to weed out duplicate files to keep your library from getting overcrowded.

The chapter also covers using folders in iTunes: how to import them; consolidate your library; and work with folders to organize the apps you use on your iPod Touch, iPhone, or iPad. And because the whole point of a well-organized library is helping you find things, you'll read about how to search your iTunes library for specific content.

Organizing Your iTunes Library

Within your computer's storage system, iTunes keeps your music and other media files in folders. Within iTunes itself, however, you'll find folders associated only with playlists and apps. For videos, music, and other audio files (like podcasts and audiobooks), iTunes uses tags to organize, find, and display your collection. Tags give information about a particular track or video. For example, when you purchase an album in the iTunes Store, you download information about each song to your computer along with the music, so iTunes knows the album, artist, and order for each song and can keep your music collection organized. This section shows you how to use tags to organize your iTunes library.

Organizing Music

Because iTunes uses a tag-based system to organize your tracks, it's important to make sure you tag your music in a way that makes it easy to find what you're looking for as your iTunes library grows.

When you rip music from CDs or buy it from the iTunes Store, the tags you need to organize your music are probably already filled in as part of the process of getting the songs into your iTunes library. But if your library has music from other sources, such as artist's web pages or some other online store, that music may be missing vital tags. Besides that, you may want to change the way some of your music is tagged, perhaps adding more information to help you create specialized playlists. Read on to learn how to work with tags to get your music library organized the way you want it.

 LET ME TRY IT

Tagging Music with Essential Tags

In iTunes, three tags are essential for organizing your songs: Name, Artist, and Album. Of these, only Name is required (if iTunes doesn't know the actual title of a song, it puts a track number, such as Track 01 or Track 02 in the Name field). But it's harder to find a song when its Artist and Album fields are blank. Here's how to fill in (or edit) these tags:

1. In iTunes, select the song you want to edit.

2. Select File, Get Info to open a dialog box that lets you edit the properties for that track.

3. Click the Info tab, shown in Figure 7.1.

4. Type the tags you want into the Name, Artist, and Album fields, as appropriate.

5. Click OK to save your tags.

If you're editing tags for an entire album, don't click OK after you've edited the first track's info. Instead, click Next. iTunes fills in the info for the next track in the album so you can edit its information. When you've finished editing the tags for that album, *then* click OK to apply all your changes at once.

Here's a way to quickly edit any field that appears in a track's listing in your iTunes library. Select the track and then click the field you want to edit. It changes to a text box; type inside the text box and then click outside it (or press Enter) to save your change.

Figure 7.1 *Editing a track's tags*

Tagging Tracks with Optional Tags

As you can see in Figure 7.1, you can tag a song with a lot more information than just Name, Artist, and Album. When you're editing a track's information, consider using these options to organize your collection in different ways:

- **Album Artist**—When an album features guest artists, you can use this field to indicate the main artist for the entire album. For example, if you bought Ella Fitzgerald's jazz album *Ella and Friends,* you might list "Ella Fitzgerald & Louis Armstrong" in the Artist field for the song "Dream a Little Dream of Me" but put "Ella Fitzgerald" in the Album Artist field, because she's the artist who ties the album together. This tag can be helpful when you want to group or sort your music collection.

- **Grouping**—If you're a classical music fan, you know that long works such as symphonies get broken up into different movements. On a CD, each movement is its own, individual track, but it's also part of the whole work. For example, if you have a recording of Mozart's Jupiter Symphony, each of the four movements group together into one symphony. For this work, the Grouping field for each movement would read "Mozart: Symphony No. 41 in C major, K. 551."

- **Composer**—Use this field to indicate who wrote the work. This tag is helpful when the person who wrote the music is different from the artist or artists who perform it, such as the composer of an opera or Broadway musical or a songwriter whose work you follow (no matter who records the songs). You can group and sort to find all works by that composer or songwriter.

- **Comments**—You can use this field to write notes to yourself about a track, but you can also use it to organize your library. The Comments field is searchable, and you can include it in the rules that set up a Smart playlist. So when you add a song that would be good to include in a dance mix, for example, you can type "Dance" in the Comments field and then set up a smart-playlist rule to find songs with the word *Dance* in that field.

 To find out how to set up a Smart playlist, **see** *"Creating a Smart Playlist" (in Chapter 5, "Playing with Playlists").*

- **Genre**—This field specifies the category of music the song fits into, such as Pop, Alternative, Country, Folk, and so on. You can choose a genre from the drop-down list or type your own. This is a super-helpful tag when you want to create a playlist of a particular type of songs.

- **Year**—This field contains the year the album was produced, but you can also use it in other ways. For example, if you follow the work of a particular composer, you can organize your collection of that composer's works by using this field to indicate the year each piece was written.

- **Track Number**—These tags list the order in which a track appears on an album and the total number of tracks on that album. That's how iTunes sorts the songs on an album to preserve its organization when you look at an album in your iTunes library.

If the Track Number fields are empty, iTunes sorts the songs on that album alphabetically by name.

- **Disc Number**—When an album contains several discs, this field makes a note of that. So for a live concert album that contains two discs, for example, this field lists the first disc as Disc Number 1 of 2 and the second as Disc Number 2 of 2. As with track numbers, this lets iTunes preserve the organization of the album.

- **BPM**—*BPM* stands for beats per minute, which describes the tempo for a song: The more beats per minute, the faster the tempo. This field is handy, for example, when you want to create a smart playlist of danceable songs with a similar beat.

- **Part of a Compilation**—A check in this box indicates that multiple artists contributed to the album, such as your favorite "Greatest Hits of Disco" or "Best Opera Arias" CD.

TELL ME MORE   Media 7.1—Working with Beats per Minute

Access this audio recording through your registered Web Edition at
my.safaribooksonline.com/9780132660273/media.

Tagging Multiple Tracks Simultaneously

You don't have to tag all your tracks one by one. When a bunch of tracks need similar tags, first select the ones you want (hold down the Shift or Ctrl/Cmd key to make multiple selections). Then click File, Get Info. iTunes asks whether you're sure you want to edit track information for multiple tracks; click Yes. (You can prevent this warning box from reappearing in the future by selecting the Do Not Ask Me Again check box.)

Click the Info tab, and then proceed as you would for tagging a single track. When you tag multiple tracks, the fields you can use to create tags are a bit different, as shown in Figure 7.2. For example, when you're editing multiple tracks, you can't give all those songs the same name. As you fill in the fields, make sure that any info you fill in applies to *all* the tracks you selected. When you're finished tagging the tracks, click OK.

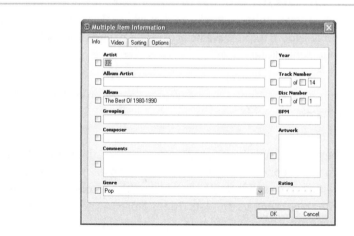

Figure 7.2   *Editing multiple tracks at once*

Organizing Videos

You tag videos—movies, TV shows, and music videos—in much the same way that you tag music. In fact, the Info tab of the dialog box that you use to tag your videos is identical to the one you use for music (see Figure 7.1)—that's because iTunes started as a source for just music before it expanded into other kinds of media. But you can add information that's specific to videos on other tabs.

Tagging Movies

When you select a movie and then select File, Get Info and click the Info tab, the dialog box that opens looks just like the one in Figure 7.1. For movies, the only essential field is Name—that's because iTunes organizes movies by their titles.

For movies that you download through the iTunes Store, the Artist field lists the director; the movie's Year and Genre fields are already filled in. But these fields are optional, and you can change them however you like. For example, if you collect movies featuring a certain actor, you might want to put that actor's name in the Artist field so that you can organize your movies by actor.

Use the Comments field to list movie ratings, such as G, PG-13, or R. Because the Comments field is searchable, you can use it to look for movies with a certain rating. This can come in handy when you're looking for a family-friendly movie to show at your daughter's slumber party.

Tagging TV Shows

When you buy or rent a TV show from the iTunes Store, here are the tags you'll find on your purchase (see Figure 7.3):

- **Name**—This field is for the name of a specific episode within a series (analogous to a specific track within an album).
- **Artist**—Here's where the name of the series goes.
- **Album Artist**—The series name also goes here, giving iTunes another field for organizing your shows.
- **Album**—This field contains the show name and its season number.

The list describes the conventions that iTunes uses when you download a TV show or series from the iTunes Store. You don't have to use these fields as just described, but if you do, it keeps your TV show information consistent. (And consistency makes for a well-organized media library.)

Figure 7.3   *Prefilled iTunes tags for an episode of a TV show*

Besides the Info tab, TV shows have information filled in on the Video tab, as Figure 7.4 shows. You'll find the following on this tab:

- **Show**—iTunes uses this field for the series name.

- **Episode ID**—This field contains a production ID for a particular episode, but you can also use it to type in the episode number. (If the Episode Number box is blank, iTunes uses this field to organize episodes within a series.)

- **Description**—For many videos you download through iTunes, this field comes already filled in with a description of the movie or TV show episode, but you can type whatever you want in this field.

- **Season Number**—iTunes uses this field to group episodes into their correct season.

- **Episode Number**—This field keeps episodes in the proper order so you can follow the developing story line.

Tagging Music Videos

iTunes organizes music videos in the same way it organizes songs. You'll find them in your music library, organized by artist and video title, as shown in Figure 7.5. You want to tag music videos the same way you tag music tracks.

Figure 7.4   *The Video tab for an episode of a TV show*

Figure 7.5   *A music video in the music library*

⊙ *To read about tagging your music tracks, **see** "Organizing Music" (earlier in this chapter).*

As Figure 7.5 shows, you can tell when a track in your Music library is a video because you can see a video icon to the right of its name.

Finding Duplicate Items

As your iTunes library grows, you're likely to end up with more than one copy of some items. For example, if you're a John Mellencamp fan, you might have two copies of the song "Jack & Diane": one from his album *American Fool,* which you ripped from the CD, and one from his greatest hits compilation, which you purchased in the iTunes Store. You don't need both copies taking up space on your computer or iPod.

 SHOW ME   Media 7.2—Finding Duplicate Items in Your iTunes Library
Access this video file through your registered Web Edition at
my.safaribooksonline.com/9780132660273/media.

You can check for duplicates in your iTunes library in two ways:

- **To find duplicate items in your library**—Go to the section of your iTunes library that you want to scour for duplicates (like Music) and select File, Display Duplicates. iTunes shows a list of items that have the same title and same artist.

- **To check for another copy of a specific item**—Select an item and hold down the Shift key as you select File, Display Exact Duplicates. If another item is an exact match, iTunes lists the duplicates.

When you're done checking for duplicates, you switch back to a view that includes all your items by clicking Show All at the bottom of the screen.

⊙ *When you find a duplicate item, you'll probably want to delete the extra file. To find out how to do that, **see** "Deleting Items from iTunes" (later in this chapter).*

Using Folders

iTunes stores your media files in folders in your computer's storage system. Most of the time, you don't have to do a thing with those folders. But at certain times you might want to work with them, such as when you're bringing an entire folder into iTunes or when you want to consolidate your media collection before you back it up. And iTunes does have folders for some kinds of content—such as playlists and apps—right inside the application. This section gets you up to speed on working with folders and iTunes.

⊙ *To find out exactly where iTunes stores your media files on your computer, **see** "Finding Music You've Imported" (in Chapter 2).*

Importing a Folder

Most of the time, you'll probably get content into iTunes by ripping CDs or through the iTunes Store. But if you've stored media files in a folder outside of iTunes and you want to bring that content into iTunes, you can do that. In fact, you've got two options for bringing a folder into iTunes—read the next two sections, then choose the method you prefer.

⊙ *You have many options for getting content into iTunes. To read about them, **see** Chapter 2, "Getting Content into iTunes."*

 LET ME TRY IT

Dragging a Folder and Its Contents into iTunes

Here's the easiest way to import a folder and all the files it holds into iTunes:

1. Open iTunes.

2. Use Windows Explorer or the Finder to find and select the folder you want.

3. Drag the folder into the Library section of your iTunes source list and drop it there.

iTunes analyzes the files in your folder and adds them to the appropriate section of your iTunes library.

 LET ME TRY IT

Importing a Folder and Its Contents into iTunes

You can also import a folder into iTunes using these steps:

1. In iTunes, select File, Add Folder to Library.

2. In the Browse for Folder dialog box, shown in Figure 7.6, find and select the folder you want to import.

Figure 7.6   *Importing a file into your iTunes library*

3.   Click OK.

As with the drag-and-drop method. iTunes analyzes the folder's contents and adds them to the appropriate section of your iTunes library.

When you import a file or folder that's stored elsewhere on your computer into iTunes, iTunes puts a shortcut to each file in the iTunes folder; the files themselves remain in their original locations.

Storing Copies of Imported Files in iTunes

As an earlier note mentions, when you import a folder into iTunes, you're importing a pointer to the folder's files, which stay in their original location. That's to save disk space on your computer. If you prefer to make a copy of files that you import into iTunes, storing those copies in your computer's iTunes folder, you can.

 LET ME TRY IT

Copying Imported Files to Your iTunes Media Folder

Here's how to tell iTunes to make a copy of any files it imports from another folder on your computer:

1.   In iTunes, select Edit, Preferences (in Windows) or iTunes, Preferences (on a Mac).

2. Click the Advanced tab, shown in Figure 7.7.

Figure 7.7   *Telling iTunes to copy files it imports into iTunes*

3. Put a check mark in the box labeled Copy Files to iTunes Media When Adding to Library.

4. Click OK.

Now iTunes will copy files, not just add shortcuts, when you import a folders or files into iTunes.

Consolidating Media Files in Your iTunes Library

Depending on how you brought your content into iTunes, you might have media files in different locations on your computer—some files might be in a folder outside the iTunes folder structure. iTunes can help you consolidate your media files, bringing copies of files stored elsewhere into iTunes. This can come in handy when you want to back up your entire iTunes library on a portable hard drive or move it to a new computer.

LET ME TRY IT

Consolidating Files in iTunes

Here's how to make sure your iTunes library has copies of all your media files:

1. In iTunes, select File, Library.

2. Choose Organize Library from the fly-out menu.

3. In the Organize Library dialog box, shown in Figure 7.8, put a check mark in the Consolidate Files box.

4. Click OK.

Figure 7.8 *Consolidating files in your iTunes library*

When you consolidate files, a copy of every media file that iTunes uses gets put in your computer's iTunes Media folder. The original files are unaffected.

Working with Folders for Apps in iTunes

Within iTunes, you can create and use folders for your playlists and the apps you use on your iPod Touch, iPhone, or iPad. Chapter 5 covers using folders with your playlists; this section focuses on your apps.

To read all about using folders to store your iTunes playlists, ***see*** *"Organizing Playlists into Folders" (in Chapter 5).*

 SHOW ME   Media 7.3—Creating and Using Apps Folders in iTunes

Access this video file through your registered Web Edition at
my.safaribooksonline.com/9780132660273/media.

LET ME TRY IT

Creating an Applications Folder in iTunes

You can create apps folders on your portable device by dragging one app icon on top of another. But did you know that you can also create folders for your apps right in iTunes? Here's how:

1. Use the USB cable that came with your device to connect it to your computer. If it's not already open, iTunes opens automatically.

2. In iTunes, select your device (under Devices) in the left source list.

3. iTunes shows information about your device in the main window. At the top of the screen, click Apps.

4. iTunes displays the apps currently loaded on your device, as shown in Figure 7.9.

Figure 7.9 *An iPhone's apps listed in iTunes*

5. Create a folder by clicking an app, dragging it on top of another app that you want in the same folder, and dropping it there.

6a. iTunes places the two apps in a folder and suggests a name for the folder, based on the apps you've put together, as shown in Figure 7.10. If you want to change the folder's name, type your preferred name in the text box.

Folder name   Folder contents   Folder

Figure 7.10 *Creating a new folder for your apps*

6b. If everything looks good, click anywhere on the representation of your device's screen to create the folder.

Managing Your Apps Folders in iTunes

You can also use iTunes to manage the apps you have in folders on your device. Here's what you do:

- **Add an app to an existing folder**—Click the app you want to put inside the folder, drag it to the folder you want, and drop it in place.

A folder can hold up to 12 apps. Nested folders don't work with apps—in other words, you can't put a folder inside another folder.

- **Open a folder**—Double-click the folder you want to open. It changes to look like the folder in Figure 7.10, showing full-size versions of the app icons it holds.

- **Remove an app from an existing folder**—Open a folder, click the app you want to remove, and drag it outside the folder.

If you want to move an app from one folder to another, you open the folder, drag the app to its new folder, and drop it there.

- **Rename a folder**—Open the folder so that it looks like the one in Figure 7.10. Click inside the text box to edit the folder's name. When you're finished, press Enter or click outside the text box.

- **Rearrange apps in a folder**—Open the folder and then drag and drop its apps' icons into their new arrangement.

- **Delete an app that's inside a folder**—Open the folder and point at the app to select it. An *x* appears in its upper-left corner; click the *x* to delete the app.

Use the same method to delete any app that's not stored inside a folder: Point at the app and click its upper-right *x*.

- **Close a folder**—Click anywhere outside an open folder to close it.

- **Delete a folder**—Open the folder and remove its apps.

After you've made whatever changes you want to your apps and their folders, click the Apply button in the lower-right part of the iTunes screen (see Figure 7.10). iTunes syncs with your device, applying the changes you made in iTunes.

If you've been fooling around with apps and folders in iTunes and you decide that you don't like the changes you made, click the lower-right Revert button. iTunes reverts to the configuration you started with.

Be aware, however, that you can't revert to an older configuration after you've synced iTunes and your device and applied the changes.

Finding What You're Looking For

As your library grows, it can get harder to find a particular item by browsing the different iTunes views. For example, what if you have a song running through your head and you want to hear it, but you're not sure who the artist is or you just can't remember which album it's on? This section shows you how to zero in on the content you want, when you want it.

SHOW ME   Media 7.4—Searching Your iTunes Library
Access this video file through your registered Web Edition at
my.safaribooksonline.com/9780132660273/media.

LET ME TRY IT

Searching for Content in Your iTunes Library

When you know some information about the item you want, you can find that item by searching your library. Here's how:

1. In your iTunes library, go to the section you want to search, such as Music.

2. In the upper-right Search box, shown in Figure 7.11, start typing your search term. You can search for all or part of a song or album title, an artist's name, a genre, and so on. You can also combine different kinds of search terms, such as an artist's name and part of a song title.

3. As you type, iTunes searches, showing possible matches even when you've put only a few characters in the Search box. Keep an eye on the results list, in case you spot the object of your search.

4. If you still have a lot of results after you've typed in your search term, scroll through the results list. When you find the item you want, click it to select it.

5. When you're finished, go back to showing all items in your library by pressing Esc or clearing the Search box. (To clear the Search box, click the x on its right side.)

Going to the Current Song

If you're listening to music as you shop in the iTunes Store or do something else in iTunes, you can easily locate the song that's currently playing. When a song comes on and you want to jump to its location, select View, Go to Current Song. To move even quicker, press Ctrl+L (in Windows) or Cmd-L (on a Mac). iTunes switches to list view, with the currently playing song selected.

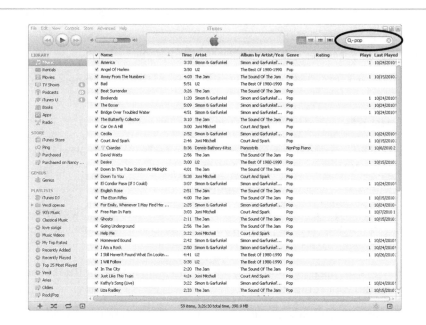

Figure 7.11   *Searching your Music library*

When you remove a song from your iTunes library, that song also gets removed from your iPod, iPhone, or iPad the next time you sync your device with iTunes.

Finding an Item's Location

When you want to find out where iTunes has stored a specific item on your computer (maybe you want to view the folder's other contents, for example), select the item and choose File, Show in Windows Explorer (on a PC) or File, Show in Finder (on a Mac). Alternatively, press Ctrl+Shift+R (on a PC) or Cmd-R (on a Mac). Your computer goes to the folder where the item is stored.

Deleting Items from iTunes

Sometimes you need to weed out items you no longer want in your iTunes library. You might want to save space, for example, by removing duplicate items (as when you import the same song from an artist's album and a movie soundtrack). You might find that your tastes have changed and you no longer listen to some of the music you used to. The same goes for videos and other content that you downloaded but no longer want in iTunes.

To delete an item from iTunes, select the copy you want to delete and use one of these methods:

- Press the Backspace or Delete key.

- Right-click (Ctrl-click on a Mac) the item. From the context menu, select Delete.

- Select Edit, Delete (in Windows) or iTunes, Delete (on a Mac).

iTunes displays a dialog box asking whether you really want to delete the item; click Remove. When you do, iTunes asks what you want to do with the file you're deleting. Choose one of the options shown in Figure 7.12:

- **Move to Recycle Bin/Trash**—Click this button if you want to get rid of the file completely, deleting it from your computer the next time you empty your Recycle Bin/Trash.

- **Keep File**—Click this button to remove the item from your iTunes library but not from your computer.

- **Cancel**—If you change your mind, you can click this button to leave the file as it is.

Figure 7.12 *Deleting a file from iTunes and your computer*

To learn more about syncing your portable device with your iTunes library, *see* "Syncing Your iPod, iPhone, or iPad with iTunes" (in Chapter 9, "Syncing and Sharing").

To delete multiple items at once, hold down the Shift key (to select a range of items) or the Ctrl/Cmd key (to select multiple items one by one) as you click the items you want to delete. Then use one of the deletion methods listed previously in this section to remove them at once. Just make sure that you want to handle all the selected items in the same way—that is, don't use this method if you want to remove some files but not others from your computer.

You put a lot of time and effort into building your iTunes library. Make sure it's well managed so you can enjoy it to the utmost.

8

Managing Your iTunes Library

As you add music and video to your iTunes library, that library grows in both value and size. To get the most out of it, pay some attention to the library as a whole. In this chapter, you'll learn how to back up all or part of your library. Whether you want to burn your favorite playlist to a CD or back up the whole thing, it's always a good idea to have copies of your files in case you need to restore those files some-day.

Media files can crowd your hard drive, taking up space on your computer and affecting its performance. This chapter shows you how to move the folder that con-tains your iTunes library to a different hard drive (this can be a different drive in your system or an external hard drive) and use it from there.

Finally, because different people have different tastes, you'll see how to create mul-tiple iTunes libraries for a single account. You'll never have to sort through your spouse's jazz albums to find your favorite country music again (or vice versa).

Burning a CD or DVD

When you transfer copies of your iTunes files to a CD or DVD, it's called *burning* a disc. This can be a good way to save your playlists (and listen to them on a CD player) or back up an album you purchased through the iTunes Store. You can even back up your entire iTunes library on DVD.

 TELL ME MORE　　Media 8.1—Copyright and Fair Use

Access this audio recording through your registered Web Edition at
my.safaribooksonline.com/9780132660273/media.

In early 2009, the iTunes Store stopped selling DRM-protected music. DRM, which stands for *digital rights management*, is a technology that restricts access to music files to prevent unauthorized copies and protect the interests of copyright holders. DRM is unpopular because it can restrict use of music that people purchased legitimately.

When the iTunes Store switched to DRM-free music (thanks to agreements with the major record labels), iTunes Plus, an AAC format, became its new standard format. You can burn iTunes Plus songs to CD as many times as you like; sync them to your iPod, iPhone, and/or iPad; and play them on any iTunes-compatible computer you own. If you purchased music before iTunes Plus became the standard, however, or if you import music from another source, that music may be DRM-protected. You can upgrade non–iTunes Plus songs that you bought through the iTunes Store (at a cost of 30 cents per song). From the iTunes Store home page, click the iTunes Plus link on the right to open a page that shows which of your songs are eligible for upgrading.

Do You Have the Right Equipment?

Before you start burning CDs and DVDs from your iTunes library, make sure you have the equipment you need:

- **A computer with a disc drive that's capable of recording to CDs and DVDs**—If your computer has an internal recordable disc drive, you should be all set. Some, but not all, external disc drives (the kind you connect to your computer via a cable) can do this.

If you use a Mac, you need an Apple Combo drive (to burn audio files to a CD) or an Apple SuperDrive (to burn audio files to a disc or back up your whole library on DVD).

- **A blank recordable disc**—Make sure you have a disc that you can record to. You can purchase discs at an office supply store (or in the office supply section of your favorite discount store). You'll find a bewildering number of options. Here's what they mean:
- **CD-R**—This is a compact disc that allows you to record music and other data files (the R stands for *recordable*). It's a good bet for recording music, because most CD players know how to read this type of disc. Each disc can be used only once for recording.

- **CD-RW**—This is a rewritable compact disc; it can be erased and reused. Unlike CD-R discs, though, these may not play in some stereos and computers.

- **DVD-R**—This is a recordable digital versatile disc (sometimes DVD stands for *digital video disc,* but these discs can hold other kinds of data, not just video). After you've burned data to a DVD-R, you're done—you can't record over that data. As you'll read in the next section, DVDs have a much greater storage capacity than CDs.

- **DVD-RW**—This is a rewritable DVD. You can erase its contents and rerecord it up to a thousand times. If you're using DVDs to back up your library, this is a good choice because you can use the same discs for periodic backups.

Be aware that any DVDs you burn from iTunes will work only in a computer; they won't play in a regular DVD player.

To find out which kind of disc you're using, check the packaging it came in.

How Much Data Can You Fit on a Disc?

When you're planning to burn a CD or DVD, it's helpful to know how many songs and other media files you can fit on a disc—you don't want to run out of space before your playlist runs out of songs.

Start by creating the playlist you want to copy (this is a necessary step in burning a disc). When you know the size of your playlist, you'll be able to estimate whether it will fit on a single disc—or whether you'll need more than one to hold it.

G *To read how to set up a playlist in iTunes, **see** "Creating a Playlist" (in Chapter 5, "Playing with Playlists").*

Next, understand how the kind of disc you're using and the kind of files you're copying affect how much you can burn onto a disc. Different kinds of disc have different storage capacities:

- **CD-R and CD-RW**—The standard size for compact discs is 12cm across (although 8cm mini-discs are also available). Twelve-centimeter CDs come in two storage capacities (check the packaging to see how much data your disc can hold):

- **650MB**—Holds up to 74 minutes of audio

- **700MB**—Holds up to 80 minutes of audio

The difference between 650MB and 700MB CDs is that tracks of the larger-capacity disc are coiled more tightly, giving the disc a larger recordable area—about two songs' worth.

- **DVD-R and DVD-RW**—A typical DVD has a storage capacity of 4.7GB (that's about five to six times the storage space a CD offers).

The kind of files you're copying also affects how much music or other data a disc can hold:

- **Lossless audio files**—If you're burning a CD to play its music in a CD player, you get the best sound quality with lossless files, which retain all the data of the original recording. But this also makes the files bigger. Files you import into iTunes using the AIFF (for Macs) or WAV (for Windows) format have the best-quality sound when you burn those files to a CD.

⊙ *To choose the right audio format for your purposes when you import music into iTunes,* **see** *"Adjusting Your CD Import Settings" (in Chapter 2, "Getting Content into iTunes").*

- **MP3 files**—These compressed files are lossy, which means they take up less space than lossless files, but at the cost of some sound quality. That said, most listeners find MP3s perfectly acceptable for listening. MP3 files require about 1MB of disc space per minute of music, which means you can fit hundreds of songs in this format onto a single disc—about 12 hours' worth of music!

- **Video files**—A two-hour movie takes up about 1.5GB of space.

When you purchase movies from the iTunes Store, you can transfer that movie to up to five authorized computers, sync it with any iPod you own, and burn it to DVD for backup purposes only. You can't burn a movie to DVD and play that disc in a DVD player. If you have Apple TV, however, you can use Apple TV to watch the movie.

To estimate whether your playlist will fit on one disc, open the playlist by clicking its name in the left source list. Look at the bottom of the track list. As Figure 8.1 shows, you can see both the playing time and the size (in megabytes or gigabytes) of the playlist. Use this information to determine how many discs you'll need to record the whole playlist (or whether you want to trim the playlist to fit on a single disc):

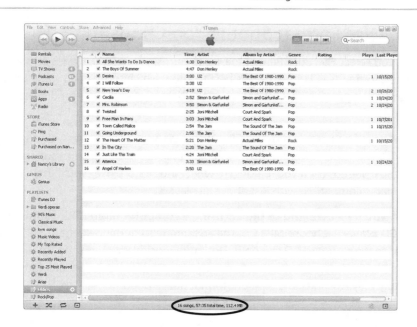

Figure 8.1 *Checking a playlist's size*

- **If you're recording an audio CD**—Use the playlist's *length* (how many hours, minutes, and seconds of music) to determine whether it will fit on a single CD: either 74 or 80 minutes. Check your CD packaging to see the capacity of your disc.

> When you're calculating the length of your playlist, be sure to add about a minute to the total to account for gaps between songs.

- **If you're recording an MP3 CD or a back-up DVD**—Look at the *size* of the playlist in megabytes or gigabytes to figure out how many files you can fit onto the disc. If you're recording to a compact disc, the disc can hold up to either 650MB or 700MB. If you're recording to a DVD, it can hold about 4.7GB.

If your playlist has more music than will fit onto a single CD, iTunes pauses during the burn process and asks whether you want to burn the playlist onto multiple CDs. If that's what you want, click **Audio CDs** to continue. iTunes fits as many complete songs as possible onto the first disc. When that disc is full, it asks you to insert another disc to continue recording.

Ⓖ For a step-by-step account of the process of burning a CD, **see** "Burning an Audio CD" (later in this chapter).

Which Disc Format Should You Choose?

When you select File, Burn Playlist to Disc to burn a CD or DVD, iTunes asks you to choose a format (see Figure 8.2). It's best to know which format you want before you begin the process. This list gives you the best format choices for different purposes:

- **If you'll be listening to the CD using a standard CD player**—Choose Audio CD. This is the format to use if you plan to listen to the disc in your car or on most stereos (or if you're not sure what kind of CD player you'll use—this format is compatible with just about all players).

- **If you'll be listening to the CD using a computer or an MP3-compatible CD player**—Choose MP3 CD. The advantage to burning songs in MP3 format is that a standard CD can hold a lot more music. When you choose this format, iTunes burns only those songs in the playlist that are in MP3 format—any playlist songs in a different format get skipped.

Songs that you buy from the iTunes Store are in AAC format. If you try to burn AAC files to an MP3 CD, iTunes skips them. If you want to burn AAC files to a CD, your best choice is Audio CD.

- **If you're backing up your music library**—Choose Data CD. This option burns all files on the playlist, no matter what their format. It also lets you record to a high-capacity DVD.

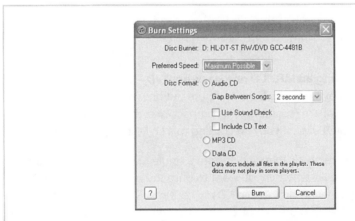

Figure 8.2 *Choosing burn settings*

What's the Best Recording Speed?

Another setting to consider before you burn a disc is the speed at which the disc will record. You select this from the Preferred Speed drop-down list in the Burn Settings dialog box (see Figure 8.2). How fast you can burn a CD depends on the discs you're using, the speed of your recorder, and how much data you're recording. At single speed (1X), a recorder writes about 176KB of audio data per second to the CD. For each increment above that, multiply 176KB by the writing speed. So 2X writes 352KB of data per second, 4X writes about 704KB of data per second, and so on, all the way up to 24X, which writes about 4.2MB of data per second—or about three minutes to fill up an 80-minute disc.

Most of the time, Maximum Possible (the default) is the setting you want you want in the Preferred Speed drop-down list. When you select this recording speed, iTunes checks the blank CD's rating and picks the optimal recording speed for that rating. But if you're having trouble recording a CD, you might try a slower speed. (Check the packaging to see the speed your disc is rated for.)

Creating a Playlist

Before you burn a CD or DVD, you must create an iTunes playlist that holds the files you want to copy. Make sure that each song you want to record has a check mark to the left of its name.

Ⓒ *Not sure how to set up a playlist in iTunes?* **See** *"Creating a Playlist" (in Chapter 5).*

If your playlist includes an audiobook from Audible.com that has chapter markers, each chapter gets burned as a separate track on the CD.

Copying Files to a CD or DVD

Now that you've done all the prep work and created a playlist, you're ready to burn that playlist to a disc.

 SHOW ME   Media 8.2—Saving an iTunes Playlist to an Audio CD
Access this video file through your registered Web Edition at
my.safaribooksonline.com/9780132660273/media.

LET ME TRY IT

Burning an Audio CD

To copy a playlist's files to an audio CD, take these steps:

1. In iTunes, go to the Playlists section of the left source list and select the playlist you want to save to a disc.

2. Insert a blank disc into your computer's CD drive.

3. Select File, Burn Playlist to Disc.

4. In the Burn Settings dialog box, shown in Figure 8.2, choose Audio CD as the Disc format.

5. Choose your settings:

   • **Preferred Speed**—You probably want the default of Maximum Possible here.

   • **Gap Between Songs**—The default is a two-second pause between the end of one song and the beginning of the next. You can pick no gap or add a gap of from one to five seconds.

   If you've made an album gapless (see Chapter 2), as you might do for a live concert album, select None from the Gap Between Songs drop-down list to make the CD copy gapless, too.

   • **Use Sound Check**—Songs are recorded at different volumes, but you don't want your playlist to be too loud for one song and too soft for the next. Put a check mark in the Use Sound Check box to even out the volume of the songs on your playlist.

   • **Include CD Text**—Some CD players can display the artist and song title for the track currently playing. If you want that info to show on the player, turn on this check box.

6. Click Burn. The recording process can take several minutes.

7. When iTunes has finished recording, eject the CD from your computer.

After you've burned an audio CD, test it by playing it in a CD player.

If your playlist requires multiple CDs to hold all its songs, only the last CD burned will include track information: song title, artist, and album. On the previous CDs, songs are identified by track number: such as Track 01, Track 02, Track 03, and so on.

 LET ME TRY IT

Burning an MP3 CD

The process for burning a CD of MP3 files is almost identical to the process for burning an audio CD, except that you have fewer settings to choose from. When you're creating a playlist to save as an MP3 CD, keep in mind that iTunes skips any songs that aren't in MP3 format as it copies files to the CD.

To burn an MP3 CD, follow these steps:

1. In iTunes, go to the Playlists section of the left source list and select the playlist you want to save to a disc.

2. Insert a blank disc into your computer's CD drive.

3. Select File, Burn Playlist to Disc.

4a. In the Burn Settings dialog box, shown in Figure 8.2, choose MP3 CD as the Disc format. (When you select this option, the settings specific to audio CDs become inactive.)

4b. If you want, choose a recording speed from the Preferred Speed drop-down list. In most cases, the default (Maximum Possible) is the best choice.

5. Click Burn. The recording process can take several minutes.

6. When iTunes has finished recording, eject the CD from your computer and test it in an MP3-compatible CD player.

 LET ME TRY IT

Burning a Data CD or DVD

You can use iTunes to create data discs that contain all the files in a playlist, no matter what kinds of files they are. Be aware, though, that data CDs and DVDs may not play in some disc players. These are best used for backup.

Here's how to burn a data disc of an iTunes playlist:

1. In iTunes, go to the Playlists section of the left source list and select the playlist you want to save to a disc.

2. Insert a blank disc into your computer's CD/DVD drive.

3. Select File, Burn Playlist to Disc.

4a. In the Burn Settings dialog box, shown in Figure 8.2, choose Data CD or DVD as the Disc format. (When you select this option, the settings specific to audio CDs become inactive.)

4b. If you want, choose a recording speed from the Preferred Speed drop-down list. In most cases, the default (Maximum Possible) is the best choice.

5. Click Burn. The recording process can take several minutes.

6. When iTunes has finished recording, eject the CD from your computer.

Troubleshooting Disc Burning

Having difficulty burning your playlist to a disc? Try these troubleshooting tips:

- **Make sure you're burning a playlist**—You can burn only a playlist of songs. You can't burn a disc from your iPod, your library, or the radio.

- **Check your playlist**—Make sure that all the songs you want to burn have a check mark beside them.

- **Shorten your playlist**—If your playlist is too long to fit on a single disc, iTunes warns you and gives you the option of canceling the burn. If you want the playlist on one disc, delete songs until its length (indicated at the bottom of the screen) is either 73 or 79 minutes or less, depending on the kind of CD you're using.

- **Choose the correct format**—If you try to burn songs in a format other than MP3 to an MP3 CD, iTunes just skips those songs.

- **Upgrade your songs**—If you're using older, DRM-protected versions of songs that your purchased from the iTunes Store before January 2009, those songs have copying restrictions. For pre–iTunes Plus songs, you can burn an unchanged playlist only up to seven times, no more.

- **Slow down the burn speed**—iTunes knows that you're impatient and tries to choose the fastest possible burn speed. But if your burner or the disc in it can't handle that speed, the burn could fail.

Backing Up Your iTunes Library

Everyone who works with computers has heard it a million times: Back up your data. Good advice—but do you follow it?

You should, especially with your iTunes library, which probably represents a significant investment of your time and money. If your computer crashed tomorrow and you lost your iTunes library, how much would it cost to replace all your music and videos? How much time would it require to reconstruct your library? Back up now, and you won't have to worry about answering those questions.

Saving Your Library to CDs or DVDs

One way to back up your iTunes library is to save it to disc—or to a whole stack of discs, if your library is large. Label the discs and store them in a place where you can easily find them if you need them.

In iTunes, select File, Library and choose Back Up to Disc from the fly-out menu. This opens the iTunes Backup Wizard, shown in Figure 8.3. The wizard walks you through the process of backing up your files to discs. It offers these choices:

- **Back Up Entire iTunes Library and Playlists**—This option saves your whole library on discs: stuff you've bought through the iTunes Store, songs you've ripped from CDs or imported from a band's website—everything. If you have a lot of media files, backing up your whole library on CDs or DVDs can take a tower of discs and a good amount of time. But if you don't have an external hard drive or other high-capacity storage medium, it's worth the effort to make sure you have backups.

- **Back Up Only iTunes Store Purchases**—This option finds songs, albums, and other content that you've bought from the iTunes Store and saves only those files to the CDs or DVDs you're burning. You might choose this option if your iTunes library contains a lot of songs that you ripped from CDs and you still have those CDs.

- **Only Back Up Items Added or Changed Since Last Backup**—This is called an *incremental backup*, and it can save you time. iTunes checks for new files and copies only those that have arrived in your library since your last backup. You can use this option (select its check box) whether you're backing up the whole library or just iTunes Store purchases.

- **Preferred Speed**—As with other disc-burning methods, you probably want to let iTunes handle this option. Leaving Maximum Possible for this setting lets iTunes determine the best recording speed for your equipment.

Figure 8.3 *The iTunes Backup wizard*

After you've selected what you want to back up, insert a blank disc in your CD/DVD drive and click the Back Up button. When that disc is full and you need to insert another, iTunes pauses and lets you know.

Backing Up Your Library on a Different Hard Drive

If you don't want to sit at your computer all day inserting and ejecting discs to back up your iTunes library, you can save a backup to another hard drive—either a different drive on your computer or an external hard drive that's connected to your computer.

 LET ME TRY IT

Backing Up to a Different Hard Drive

Performing this kind of backup is simple. If you're using an external hard drive, first make sure that it's connected to your computer. Then take these steps:

1. In Windows Explorer or the Finder, locate your iTunes folder.

   *If you're not sure where to find your iTunes folder on your computer, **see** "Finding Music You've Imported" (in Chapter 2).*

2. Locate the drive where you want to store your backup.

3. Drag the iTunes folder to the other drive and drop it there.

Your computer copies the iTunes folder—and all its contents—to the drive where you dropped it. If your iTunes library is large, the backup may take a while. Be patient. You want to make sure that all your files and playlists are copied.

Restoring Your Library from a Backup

If a computer catastrophe strikes, you may need to restore all those files you backed up. (That's why you backed them up in the first place, right?) Or you may want to transfer your library to a new computer. Whether you backed up your library on discs or on a different hard drive, restoration is easy.

Restoring Your Library from Backup CDs or DVDs

To restore your library from your backup discs, open iTunes and insert the first disc into your computer's CD/DVD drive. A message appears asking whether you want to restore your library. Select Overwrite Existing Files and click Restore to start the process. Just as it took some time to back up your library to discs, it takes time to copy your backed-up files from the discs to the computer.

 LET ME TRY IT

Restoring Your Library from a Backup on Another Hard Drive

When you've stored a backed-up library on another hard drive, here's how to restore your library in iTunes:

1. If iTunes is open, close it.

2. Find your iTunes folder on your computer and open it.

   🄖 *To find where your iTunes folder is stored on your computer, **see** "Finding Music You've Imported" (in Chapter 2).*

3. In your iTunes folder, select the file iTunes Music Library.xml and drag it to your computer's Desktop.

4. In your iTunes folder, select the following file and drag it to your computer's Recycle Bin (Windows) or Trash (Mac):
   - In Windows: iTunes Library.itl
   - On a Mac: iTunes Library

5. Start up iTunes.

6. Select Files, Library and choose Import Playlist from the fly-out menu.

7. In the Import dialog box, shown in Figure 8.4, navigate to your computer's Desktop and select iTunes Music Library.xml.

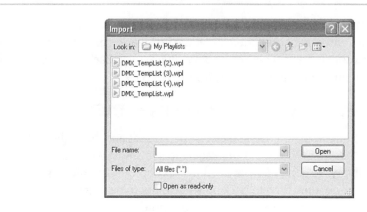

Figure 8.4   *The Import dialog box*

8. Click Open (Windows) or Choose (Mac).

iTunes re-creates your library. The next time you sync your iPod or other portable device with iTunes, the device completely resyncs with your restored library (so the operation could take some time).

⊙ *To read more about getting your portable device and iTunes in sync, **see** "Syncing Your iPod, iPhone, or iPad with iTunes" (in Chapter 9, "Syncing and Sharing").*

 LET ME TRY IT

Restoring Podcasts to Your Library

If you go through the steps to restore your iTunes library and notice that the podcasts you saved are missing, here's how to fix the problem:

1. In iTunes, select File, Add Folder to Library (in Windows) or File, Add to Library (on a Mac).

2. In the dialog box that opens, browse to find your iTunes folder and click the folder to open it.

3. Inside the iTunes folder, find the iTunes Music folder and click to open it.

4. Inside the iTunes Music folder, find and select the Podcasts folder.

5. Click OK (in Windows) or Choose (on a Mac) to restore your podcasts.

Moving Your iTunes Media Folder

When you install iTunes, the installer creates a system of folders on your computer to hold your iTunes library. The iTunes folder holds a number of nested subfolders to organize the different kinds of content you have in your library. In iTunes 9 and later, your iTunes folder contains these subfolders:

*   iTunes Media

*   Audiobooks

*   Automatically Added to iTunes

*   Books

*   iPod Games

*   iTunes U

*   Mobile Applications

*   Movies

*   Music

*   Podcasts

*   Ringtones

*   TV Shows

*   Voice Memos

If you're upgrading to iTunes 10 from iTunes 8 or earlier, you can keep your library better organized and make sharing between computers easier by upgrading to iTunes Media organization.

In iTunes, select File, Library, Organize Library. In the Organize Library dialog box, select the Upgrade to iTunes Media Organization check box. Click OK to reorganize your files. (If you don't see that check box, you're already using iTunes Media organization.)

You can choose where you store your iTunes Media folder. This can be helpful when your hard drive is full of all those media files you've imported and you want to move them to a different hard drive on your system to free up space on the main drive.

When you move your iTunes Media folder to a different location, you can keep your playlists, ratings, and play history intact. Doing so requires two steps:

- **Telling iTunes to keep your iTunes Media folder organized**—iTunes organizes your music by artist. Every album and track by the same artist goes into a folder labeled with that artist's name. Folders also exist for compilation albums and unknown artists. Turning on this option ensures a smooth move to the Media folder's new home.

  (G) *When you let iTunes handle the organization of your iTunes Media folder, you can focus on organizing your collection through tags. **See** "Organizing Your iTunes Library" (in Chapter 7, "Organizing Your Content") for more information about tags.*

- **Moving the folder**—The methods are slightly different for Windows and Mac users because of differences in how the operating systems work.

SHOW ME   Media 8.3—Moving Your iTunes Media Folder
Access this video file through your registered Web Edition at
my.safaribooksonline.com/9780132660273/media.

The next three sections walk you through the process of moving your iTunes Media folder.

LET ME TRY IT

Preparing to Move Your iTunes Media Folder

Before you can move your iTunes Media folder, take these steps to prepare your library for the move:

1. In iTunes, select Edit, Preferences (in Windows) or iTunes, Preferences (on a Mac).

2. Click Advanced (see Figure 8.5).

3. Select the box labeled Keep iTunes Media Folder Organized.

4. Click OK.

That gets your iTunes Media folder set up. How you proceed depends on whether your computer runs on Windows or Mac OS X.

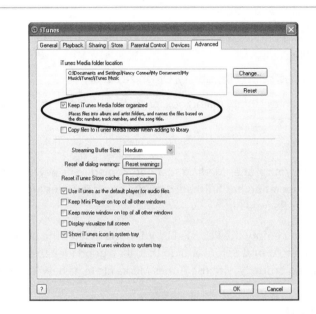

Figure 8.5 *Keeping the iTunes Media folder organized in preparation of moving it*

 LET ME TRY IT

Moving Your iTunes Media Folder: Windows

If your computer uses Windows as its operating system, follow these steps to move your iTunes Media Folder to a different hard drive:

1. In iTunes, select Edit, Preferences.

2. Click the Advanced tab, shown in Figure 8.5.

3. At the top of the dialog box, you can see the current location of your iTunes Media folder. Click the Change button to its right.

4. A dialog box opens that lets you browse the folders on your computer. Navigate to the location where you want to move your iTunes Media folder (such as a different hard drive).

5. Click Make New Folder.

6. Windows creates a new folder; type in the name for your new iTunes Media folder.

7. Click OK to save the new folder.

8. Back in iTunes, the Advanced tab shows a new location for your iTunes Media folder. Click OK.

9. Still in iTunes, select File, Library, Organize Library.

10. In the Organize Library dialog box, put a check mark in the Consolidate Files box.

11. Click OK.

12. Wait while your iTunes Media folder gets copied to its new location. When the copy operation has finished, drag the original iTunes Media folder to your computer's Recycle Bin.

The next time you empty the Recycle Bin, Windows deletes the old iTunes Media folder and all its contents. Before you do that, it's a good idea to make sure that iTunes is working properly with the iTunes Media file in its new location.

 LET ME TRY IT

Moving Your iTunes Media Folder: Mac

If you use a Mac, these instructions are for you. Open iTunes and then follow these steps:

1. Select iTunes, Preferences.

2. In the Preferences window, click Advanced.

3. At the top of the Advanced window, find the current location of your iTunes Media folder. Click the Change button to its right.

4. The Change Media Folder Location window opens. Browse to the location where you want your new iTunes Media folder.

5. Click New Folder.

6. The New Folder window opens; type in the name for new iTunes Media folder.

7. Click Create to create the new folder.

8. Back in the Change Media Folder Location window, click Choose.

9. Back in the Advanced window, click OK.

10. In iTunes, select File, Library, Organize Library.

11. In the Organize Library dialog box, put a check mark in the Consolidate Files box.

12. Click OK.

13. Wait while your iTunes Media folder gets copied to its new location. When the copy operation has finished, drag the original iTunes Media folder to the Trash.

The next time you empty the Trash, your computer deletes the old iTunes Media folder and all its contents. Before you do that, it's a good idea to make sure that iTunes is working properly with the iTunes Media file in its new location.

Working with Multiple Libraries

When several people share a computer, it doesn't mean they share musical tastes. You might be a country music fan, for example, but your spouse is crazy about opera, your daughter loves alternative rock, and your son listens to nothing but hip-hop. When you all store your music in a single iTunes library, that kind of variety can get unwieldy. One solution is to create multiple iTunes libraries—one for each user to store his or her tunes. You can name your new iTunes library (the folder containing all of your iTunes content and the iTunes Library file) whatever you like and store it wherever you like.

If you have a lot of movies, you know that each one takes up a good deal of space on your hard drive. To free up some room on your computer, create a second library to hold your movies, and store that library on a high-capacity external hard drive.

 SHOW ME Media 8.4—Creating a New iTunes Library
Access this video file through your registered Web Edition at
my.safaribooksonline.com/9780132660273/media.

 **LET ME TRY IT**

Creating Multiple Libraries

Here's how to create a new library for your iTunes account:

1. If iTunes is open, close it.

2. Hold down the Shift key (in Windows) or the Opt key (on a Mac) while you start up iTunes. Keep holding down the key until you see the dialog box shown in Figure 8.6.

Figure 8.6   *Creating a new iTunes library*

3. Click Create Library.

4. In the New iTunes Library dialog box, shown in Figure 8.7, navigate to the folder where you want to store the new library.

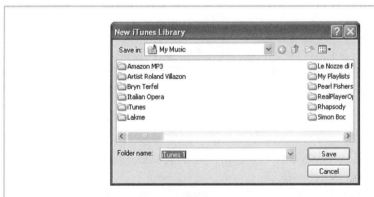

Figure 8.7   *Locating and naming a new iTunes library*

5. Type a name for your library, such as *Moms Music* or *Holiday Favorites*, the File Name field.

6. Click Save (in Windows) or OK (on a Mac).

iTunes creates your new library, giving it the name you assigned, and opens to that library. Now you can add content to that library.

⊕ **See** *Chapter 2 for everything you need to know about adding audio and video to your iTunes library.*

⊕ *Now that you've created a new library, you can share it over a network;* **see** *"Sharing Your iTunes Library" (in Chapter 9) to learn how.*

 LET ME TRY IT

Choosing a Library

When you have more than one library associated with your iTunes account, iTunes opens to the library you used most recently. The name of the current library appears at the top of the iTunes window.

If you want to switch to a different library, you have to close iTunes and open it again, following these steps:

1. Hold down the Shift key (in Windows) or the Opt key (on a Mac) while you start up iTunes. Keep holding down the key until you see the dialog box shown in Figure 8.6.

2. Click Choose Library.

3. In the dialog box that opens, shown in Figure 8.8, find and open the folder that contains the library you want. Inside the folder, select the iTunes library file.

4. Click Open (in Windows) or OK (on a Mac).

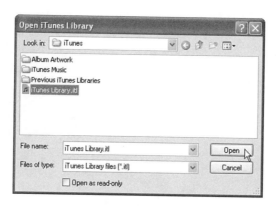

Figure 8.8   *Choosing a library to open*

Your Preferences settings—such as playback settings and parental controls—are associated with your user account, not with each library. So when you have multiple libraries for a single iTunes account, your preference settings are the same across all libraries. If you need to have different preferences for different users—for example, you want to set parental controls for your kids but don't need them for your own account—create a separate iTunes account for each user.

Part of what makes iTunes so popular is its flexibility—you can play music and video on many
devices and in many ways. This chapter shows you
how to get the most out of that flexibility.

9

Syncing and Sharing

iTunes is a great way to play, store, and manage your audio and video files, but you probably never intended to always sit in front of your computer and listen to music there. Most likely you use iTunes as a central repository for music, videos, and other entertaining and edifying content that you experience in a variety of ways: on your iPod, iPhone, or iPad; on a different computer; or through your home theater system.

This chapter shows you how to sync and share among all the devices you might use to experience the contents of your iTunes library. *Syncing* means making sure that your portable device is up-to-date with its music, playlists, videos, and other content. *Sharing* means making your iTunes library available to other computers on a network or other iTunes-compatible devices, such as Apple TV or Apple-compatible speakers.

You'll learn how to sync your iPod, iPhone, or iPad with iTunes—both automatically and manually. Because your iTunes library may have more content than your iPod has space for, you'll see how to pick and choose the content that syncs so you'll always have quick access to your favorites. You can use iTunes to sync more than the files in your iTunes library—find out how to sync personal information such as contacts, email accounts, calendars, and bookmarks. An introduction to MobileMe, Apple's subscription service for cloud-based computing, shows you how you can store information on the Web and sync with it anytime.

iTunes offers several different kinds of sharing. The simplest makes your iTunes library available to other computers on the same network; you can play music from other shared libraries on the network as well. Home Sharing takes sharing one step further, letting you import iTunes files from networked computers. And with AirPlay, new in iTunes 10, you can wirelessly stream music to AirPlay-enabled speakers throughout your home.

Syncing Your iPod, iPhone, or iPad with iTunes

When you sync your iPod, iPhone, or iPad with iTunes, you bring your device in line with your iTunes library. If you've bought a new album through the iTunes Store, for example, syncing copies that album to your device. Or if you've deleted some podcasts that you're finished with, those podcasts disappear from your device. You can sync all or part of your iTunes library—this chapter explains how to choose what you want to sync.

In addition, if you've downloaded any music, videos, books, apps, or other content to your device, syncing brings those into your iTunes library.

The first time you connected your device to your computer and set it up with iTunes, iTunes gave you the option to sync automatically. If you selected this, all you have to do to sync is connect your device to your computer. iTunes starts up automatically (if it's not already open) and gets your device in sync.

G *To read about setting up a portable device with iTunes, **see** "Setting Up Your iPod, iPhone, or iPad" (in Chapter 1, "Getting Started with iTunes 10"). If you didn't choose automatic syncing when you set up your device and want to use it now, **see** "Setting Up Automatic Syncing" (coming up in this chapter).*

You can follow the progress in the information pane at the top of the iTunes screen. It lists the steps of the sync—preparing, backing up, copying files, and so on—so you can see what it's doing. When the sync is complete (as in Figure 9.1), iTunes lets you know that it's now okay to disconnect the device. Click the Eject button (to the right of your device) and disconnect your iPod or other device from your computer.

When the sync is complete, select your device (it's under Devices in the source list) and take a look at its Summary page (see Figure 9.1) to check your device's capacity. Note the summary page's Sync button in the lower-right part of the screen. If you haven't enabled automatic syncing, click Sync to tell iTunes to sync with your device now.

Syncing makes it a snap to transfer all your music, video, and other media files to a new portable device. When you buy a new iPod, for example, it automatically syncs with your iTunes library the first time you connect it to your computer. (Chapter 1 tells you how to set up a new iPod, iPhone, or iPad with iTunes.)

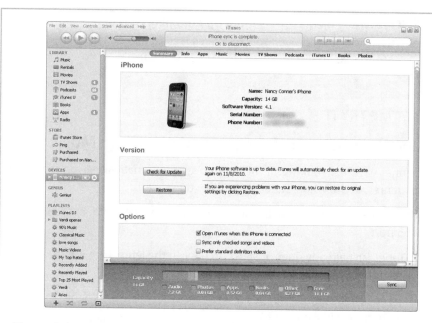

Figure 9.1 *A summary page for an iPhone*

Setting Up Automatic Syncing

The easiest way to keep your device in sync with your iTunes library is to have iTunes sync them automatically. When you connect your iPod, iPhone, or iPad to your computer, iTunes detects the device and syncs with it. Simple.

You can sync only selected libraries and playlists, or you can sync everything. If your iTunes library is larger than you have room for on your device, it makes sense to select what you want to sync—that way, you'll know that the content you want can fit on your device. This section tells you how to fine-tune automatic syncing.

If you want, you can sync by individual items. First, go through your library and uncheck any items you *don't* want to sync. Then, on your device's summary page (see Figure 9.1), turn on the check box labeled Sync Only Checked Songs and Videos. Click Apply to sync and save this setting.

Even though you can fine-tune your syncing in this way, doing so can be cumbersome. Not only does it require constant checking and unchecking of items in your library, but unchecked items won't play in your iTunes playlists (iTunes skips over any item that's not checked). A better idea is to create playlists of music that you want to play on your iPod or other device, and then sync only those playlists.

SHOW ME   Media 9.1—Setting Up Automatic Syncing
Access this video file through your registered Web Edition at
my.safaribooksonline.com/9780132660273/media.

 LET ME TRY IT

Choosing Your Settings for Automatic Syncing: Music

To tell iTunes which of your music you want to sync automatically—songs, playlists, albums, genres, or the whole shebang—follow these steps:

1. Use the cable that came with your device to connect it to your computer's USB port.

2. If iTunes isn't already open, it starts up now. In the left source list, look under Devices and select your device.

3. iTunes opens a summary page for your device. Scroll down to the Options section, shown in Figure 9.2.

4. Make sure that the check box labeled Manually Manage Music and Videos does *not* contain a check mark.

5. At the top of the screen, click Music to open the Music page, shown in Figure 9.3.

6. In the Sync Music section, choose what you want to sync:

    • **Entire Music Library**—This is a good choice if your music library will fit comfortably on your device. For example, if your music library takes up 24GB, you might choose this option for your 32GB iPod Touch, but you wouldn't want it for your 16GB iPod Nano or your 2GB iPod Shuffle.

> Not sure how big your iTunes music library is? In the source list, look under Library and click Music. This opens your music library. Look at the bottom of the screen, which shows how big the current library is in terms of number of items, time, and size (in gigabytes).

    • **Selected Playlists, Artists, Albums, and Genres**—If you want to pick and choose what syncs automatically between iTunes and your device, choose this option. Then go through the Playlists, Artists, Albums, and Genres sections, putting a check mark next to everything you want to sync automatically.

Figure 9.2 *Choosing sync options*

Figure 9.3 *Setting sync options for music*

7. Check or uncheck these boxes, as you prefer:

- **Include Music Videos**—Pretty self-explanatory. If you don't plan to watch music videos on your portable device, you don't need to have this checked.
- **Include Voice Memos**—Also self-explanatory.
- **Automatically Fill Free Space with Songs**—When you choose this option, iTunes automatically syncs as much content as possible with your device. It's a good choice for smaller-capacity devices, such as an iPod Shuffle.

8. Click Apply (circled in Figure 9.3).

iTunes syncs your device with iTunes, using the Music settings you chose. The next time you connect your device to your computer, iTunes will automatically sync with it, according to these settings.

If you have second thoughts about changing how your music library syncs, *don't* click Apply in step 8. Instead, click Revert to go back to how the settings were before you made any changes.

If you've created a smart playlist (see Chapter 5, "Playing with Playlists") that isn't syncing properly, try this: Click the smart playlist (under Playlists in the source list) to open it and make sure its tracks are arranged the way you want them. Then right-click the smart playlist and, from the context menu, select Copy to Play Order. Finally, sync your device with iTunes.

Choosing Your Settings for Automatic Syncing: Other Content

Many people want automatic syncing for music only, because they use their iPods primarily for listening to music. But you can set up automatic syncing for any kind of content you store in iTunes. So if you use your portable device to watch videos or listen to podcasts or audiobooks, you can set up those to autosync according to your preferences.

Connect your device to your computer. In iTunes, select the device (it's under Devices in the left source list). At the top of the page, click the kind of content you want to sync. When the page for that kind of content opens, check its Sync check box.

The following list describes your options for each kind of content:

- **Movies**—Movies take up a lot of space on your device, so you might not want to sync your entire collection automatically. As Figure 9.4 shows, though, you have other options. You can automatically include your newest (or oldest) unwatched movie; the movie you added to your collection most recently (whether or not you've watched it); batches of three, five, or ten movies; or everything in your collection.

As you make selections for autosyncing, keep an eye on the capacity bar at the bottom of the page; it changes to show much space the changes you're making would take up on your device. So if syncing your entire movie library, for example, pushes the video portion of the capacity bar way to the right, all those movies would take up too much space on your device. In that case, you might decide to autosync a smaller number or add movies manually (an upcoming section tells you how to do that).

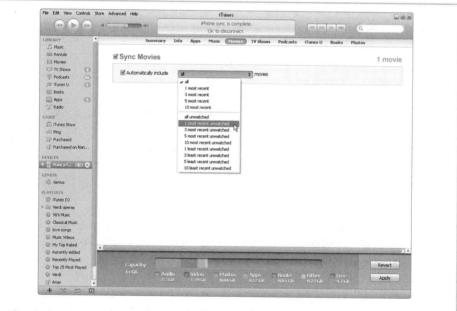

Figure 9.4 *Choosing which movies to autosync*

- **TV Shows, Podcasts, and iTunes U**—These kinds of content work similarly—they're individual units (an episode, single podcast, or lecture) that are part of a series. So iTunes handles autosyncing for TV shows, podcasts, and iTunes U courses similarly. As with movies, you can choose to sync your entire collection, or you can select a number of episodes based on how long you've had them and whether you've watched or listened to them yet. In addition, you can autosync all shows, podcasts, or courses, or only those you select.

- **Books**—This page includes two kinds of books:
  - **Audiobooks**—You can choose to sync all audiobooks or only those you select.
  - **iBooks**—If you use the iBooks app on your portable device as an e-reader for books, your iBooks also appear here. You can choose to sync only books, only PDFs, or both. In addition, you can tell iTunes to sort books by title or by author.
- **Apps**—If you find an interesting-looking app while you're browsing the iTunes Store on your computer, you can download it to iTunes and then add it to your iPod Touch, iPhone, or iPad the next time you sync. Make sure the Sync Apps box on this page is checked, and then scroll down to make sure there's also a check in the Automatically Sync New Apps check box. iTunes takes care of the rest.

ⓒ *You can also sync photos between your computer and your portable device through iTunes. **See** "Syncing Photos" (coming up in this chapter) for detailed instructions.*

What If Your Library Is Too Big to Sync?

iTunes users tend to love their music, and you may find that your iTunes library grows to contain more songs that your iPod can hold. If that happens, you'll see a message from iTunes when you try to sync, telling you that the sync can't proceed because there's not enough free space on your device to hold all the items in your library. The message asks if you want to choose a selection of songs to sync to your device. Click Yes.

iTunes creates a playlist based on your music preferences, such as song ratings and frequency of play, and names it "*Your Device's Name* Selection," with the name iTunes uses for your device in place of *Your Device's Name*. If your device appears in the source list as Jane Smith's iPod, for example, the playlist is called Jane Smith's iPod Selection. This playlist appears in the source list with your other playlists. Whenever you sync the device for which this special playlist was created, iTunes syncs the special playlist with it.

If you've set iTunes to sync movies, TV shows, or both, iTunes can't create a Selection playlist for syncing. Instead, you get an error message telling you that there's not enough space on your device to sync with your iTunes library. Click OK to get rid of the message; then turn off automatic syncing for movies or TV shows. Go back to your device's summary page and click the lower-right Sync button. Now iTunes will give you the option to create the Selection playlist when your library is too big for your device's available space.

Syncing Music and Videos Manually

If you're the type who likes to do things for yourself, you can say "No, thanks" to iTunes automatic syncing and decide for yourself which items you want to sync. Manual syncing is also the best choice when you want to use your device with more than one computer.

 LET ME TRY IT

Do-It-Yourself Syncing

Here's how to sync iTunes and your portable device by hand:

1. Connect your portable device to your computer's USB port. (iTunes starts up if it isn't already open.)

2. In the left source list, look under Devices and select your device.

3. On the device's summary page (click Summary at the top of the screen, if necessary), scroll down to the Options section (see Figure 9.2) and check the box labeled Manually Manage Music and Videos.

4. Click Apply.

5. In the Library section of the source list, select the kind of content you want to sync: Music, Movies, or TV Shows.

6. Select the content you want to sync and drag it to your device (under Devices in the source list). You can drag individual items, groups of items, playlists, albums, and so on. As soon as you drop content on your device, iTunes starts the sync.

7. When the sync has finished, click the Eject button (to the right of your device) before you disconnect it from your computer.

 LET ME TRY IT

Using Autofill

Autofill occupies a middle ground between autosyncing and manual syncing. You can use it only if iTunes is set to sync manually, but (as the name implies) Autofill automatically fills your device with music. When you connect your iPod to your computer, Autofill selects songs at random and copies them to your device. You can set criteria to help iTunes select the best songs for an Autofill.

Autofill is a great choice if you have a newer iPod Shuffle and you want to hear random songs from your collection without making the effort to choose what to put on the device. Here's how to use Autofill:

1. Connect your device to your computer.

2. In iTunes, select the device from the left source list and check its summary page to make sure that Manually Manage Music and Videos is selected (it's in the Options section).

3. In the source list, click the triangle next to your device's name to show the categories of its contents.

4. Click Music. A track list of music on your device appears. At the bottom of the list is the Autofill pane, shown in Figure 9.5.

5. Click the left Autofill From button and select the Autofill source you want. This could be a playlist, Genius, or your entire music library.

6. Click the Autofill button on the right to copy random tracks to your device.

7. When the sync has finished, click the Eject button (to the right of your device's name) before you disconnect the device.

Autofill does not work with first- and second-generation versions of the iPod Shuffle.

Autofill pane

Figure 9.5   *The Autofill pane*

LET ME TRY IT

Adjusting Your Autofill Settings

To help iTunes pick the best songs when doing an Autofill, take these steps:

1. With your device connected to your computer (and the Manually Manage Music and Videos setting turned on), find your device under Devices and click the triangle beside its name.

2. Under your device, select Music.

3. In the Autofill pane (see Figure 9.5), click the Settings button to open the Autofill Settings dialog box, shown in Figure 9.6.

4. Choose your settings:

   - **Replace All Items When Autofilling**—This option wipes your music slate clean and replaces all songs each time you Autofill. So if you have certain songs that you always want on your device, *don't* check this one.
   - **Choose Items Randomly**—If you turn off this option, Autofill adds items in the order in which they appear in your library or the playlist you selected.
   - **Choose Higher Rated Items More Often**—This option appears only if you've opted to choose items randomly. Checking it means that you'll hear songs you've marked as favorites more frequently than those you've rated lower.
   - **Reserve Space for Disk Use**—If you don't want Autofill to fill your device entirely with music, move this slider to indicate how much space you want to save.

5. When your settings look good, click OK to apply them.

The next time you sync your device using Autofill, iTunes uses your saved settings.

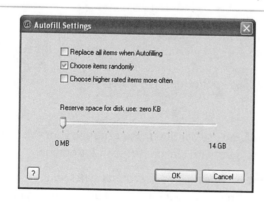

Figure 9.6   *Choosing Autofill settings*

Syncing Your Information

Your iTunes library is only the beginning of what you can sync. You can also keep the personal information that you store on your computer, laptop, and other devices in sync, too. This section shows you how.

What You Can Sync

There's no point in keeping all your contact information, notes, or favorite website bookmarks on your desktop computer at home—you might need that information when you're out and about. By using iTunes to sync such information among the various places where it might come in handy, you can make sure that you also have the information you need right at your fingertips.

If you have an iPod Classic, an iPod Nano, or an older iPod, you can sync information in one direction: from your computer to your iPod. For newer models, including the iPod Touch, iPhone, and iPad, syncing works both ways. The iPod Shuffle holds audio files, not productivity tools, so it doesn't sync contacts, calendars, and so on.

Here's what you can sync between your computer and your other devices:

- **Contacts**—Windows users can sync their contacts with Microsoft Outlook 2003 or later, Google Contacts, the Windows Address Book, or the Yahoo! Address Book. Mac users can sync using the Address Book application. If you use Microsoft Entourage, Google Contacts, or the Yahoo! Address with your Mac, you can sync those, too.

Many people sync their Outlook accounts with networking services such as LinkedIn. If you have a lot of LinkedIn connections—running in the hundreds or thousands—and you've synced those connections with Outlook, beware. In this situation, syncing Outlook with iTunes, and then syncing your iPhone contacts with iTunes, could cause performance problems for your phone.

- **Calendars**—If you use Windows, you can sync your calendar with Outlook. If you use a Mac, sync with iCal or Microsoft Entourage.

- **Mail Accounts**—Syncing email accounts syncs your account settings (email address, display name, server name, and user name) but not passwords or email messages. iTunes syncs mail accounts only one way: from your computer to your device. In Windows, you can sync email accounts with Outlook or Outlook express. On a Mac, you can sync with Mail.

- **Bookmarks**—If you use Windows, you can sync your Internet Explorer bookmarks with your device. If you use Mac, you can sync your Safari bookmarks.

- **Notes**—Windows users can sync any notes they keep in Outlook with their iPhones Notes app; Mac users can do the same for their Mail notes. (Your Mac must run on Mac OS X 10.5.7 or later to sync notes.)

 LET ME TRY IT

Using iTunes to Sync Information between Your Computer and Your iPod, iPhone, or iPad

To get your personal information in sync, follow these steps:

1. Connect your device to your computer.

2. In the left source list, find your device (under Devices) and select it.

3. When info about your device appears in the iTunes window, click Info (at the top of the screen).

4. The iTunes window changes to look something like the one shown in Figure 9.7. Put a check mark in the box for any info you want to sync:

   - **Contacts**—Choose the source of your contacts and whether you want to sync all contacts or selected groups. If you want to sync groups, put a check in the box beside each group you want to sync. When you're syncing only certain groups, you can also specify whether you want to sync contacts created outside of groups on your device to your computer, and if so, where.

   - **Calendars**—You can sync all calendars or only those you select. You can also tell iTunes not to sync calendar events that are older than a number of days that you specify (30 days is the default).

   - **Mail Accounts**—If you have multiple email accounts associated with your email program, tell iTunes which ones you want to sync.

   - **Other**—Here's where you opt to sync bookmarks, notes, or both. Put a check mark by what you want to sync and select the source.

   - **Advanced**—If you want to replace all of the contacts, calendars, mail accounts, bookmarks, and notes (or any combination of these) that are currently on your iPod Touch, iPhone, or iPad, check the box of anything you want to replace in this section. You can do this only once, during the next sync. After that, iTunes turns off the Advanced options you replaced.

5. Click Apply to sync your information.

6. When the sync has finished, click the Eject button (it's in the source list, to the right of your device's name) before you disconnect your device.

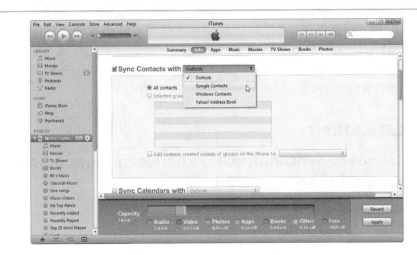

Figure 9.7 *Telling iTunes which information to sync (on Windows and syncing with an iPhone)*

Syncing Photos

iPods and other Apple portable devices make great portable photo viewers. If your iPod has a color display or you have an iPhone or iPad, you can use iTunes to add digital photos to your device.

Keep in mind a few pointers before you try syncing photos:

- The photos you're syncing must be in a format that's compatible with your device. Compatible formats in Windows are JPG, JPEG, BMP, GIF, TIF, TIFF, PSD, SGI, and PNG. For Macs, compatible formats are JPG, JPEG, BMP, GIF, TIFF, PSD, SGI, PNG, PICT, JPG2000, and JP2.

- You can't drag individual photos or groups of photos to your device through iTunes (as you can with songs). When you use iTunes to sync photos, you must sync by selecting Photos at the top of the device's page.

- Photo syncing works one way: from your computer to your device. You can't use iTunes to copy photos from your device to your computer. If you want to do that, you need to use a photo program, such as Windows Photo Gallery or iPhoto.

ⓖ *You can also stream photos from your computer to your Apple TV. **See** "Displaying Your Photos on Apple TV" (in Chapter 6, "Viewing in iTunes: TV, Movies, and More").*

SHOW ME   Media 9.2—Syncing Photos with iTunes
Access this video file through your registered Web Edition at
my.safaribooksonline.com/9780132660273/media.

LET ME TRY IT

Using iTunes to Sync Photos

If you want to use iTunes to sync photos to your portable device, here's all you have to do:

1. Connect your iPod, iPhone, or iPad to your computer.

2. In the source list's Devices section, select your device.

3. At the top of screen showing information about your device, click Photos.

4. Put a check mark in the Sync Photos From box, shown in Figure 9.8.

5. From the drop-down list, select the folder or album where you store the photos you want to sync.

6. Select the subfolders you want to sync. You can select all folders and albums, or specify individual ones that you select. As you select individual folders or albums, iTunes lists the number of photos each selection contains. The total number of photos appears in the upper-right corner (see Figure 9.8).

> As you select folders or albums for your sync, keep an eye on the Capacity bar at the bottom of the screen. When you make selections, it changes to show how much space those selections would occupy on your device. You can adjust your selections to take up more or less space, as you prefer.

7a. You may see an option to include videos in the sync (not available on all devices). If you want to sync video files as well as photos, select the Include Videos check box.

7b. You may see an option to include full-resolution photos (not available if your device is an iPod Touch, iPhone, or iPad). You want this option if you plan to transfer the photos from your iPod to a different computer; select the box labeled Include Full-Resolution Photos.

8. Click Apply to start the sync.

9. After the sync has finished, click the Eject button (to the right of your device's name in the source list) and disconnect your device.

The sync may take a few minutes, especially if you're transferring a lot of photos. Later syncs will be faster.

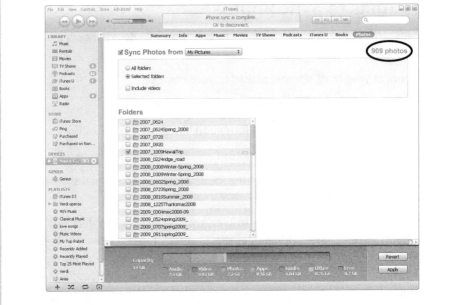

Figure 9.8   *Selecting folders for photo syncing*

Syncing in the Cloud with MobileMe

MobileMe is a subscription-based service that provides a variety of services— including email, an address book, a calendar, a photo repository, and storage—on the Web. Because your emails, photos, and other data are stored on Apple's Web servers instead of on, say, the hard drive of your desktop computer at home, you're keeping your data in "the cloud." And cloud-based data storage makes syncing your all devices and computers a snap. This section shows you how to get started with MobileMe and use it to keep your information current on all your devices.

One useful service that comes with MobileMe is called Find My iPhone (or Find My iPad, if that's the device you use). If you misplace the device, this handy feature pinpoints it on a map at www.me.com/find or by using the Find My iPhone or Find My iPad app on another device. You can also make your lost device play a sound, even if your phone is set to silent, for those times when it's playing hide-and-seek between the sofa cushions. You can also lock your phone's data, and even erase that data and restore the phone to its original settings, or display a message on the device, telling whoever finds it how to reach you—all remotely.

Find My iPhone/iPad comes with MobileMe, but Apple has also made this useful app available for free. Your device—iPhone 4, iPad, or fourth-generation iPod Touch—must be running iOS 4.2 to use this app. For set-up instructions, see "Setting Up Find My iPhone/iPad" later in this chapter.

Creating a MobileMe Account

Before you can use MobileMe, you need to set up a MobileMe account. Apple lets you try MobileMe for 60 days before charging you for the service, which costs $99 a year. To take MobileMe for a 60-day spin, go to www.apple.com/mobileme and click the Sign Up for MobileMe Free Trial button. Fill out the two-page sign-up form, which asks for information such as your preferred user name and password, your real name, and security information. You also have to provide valid credit card info (so Apple can charge you if you want to continue after your free trial) and read and accept the terms of service.

After you've created your account, you can sign in and access your apps anytime at www.me.com.

 LET ME TRY IT

Setting Up MobileMe on Your iPod Touch, iPhone, or iPad

The first step in getting MobileMe to work with your portable device is to set up the device. If you're using MobileMe with an iPod Touch or iPhone, make sure your device is up-to-date—it needs to be using iOS 4.1 or later. If you need to upgrade your device's operating system, connect the device to your computer and, in iTunes, select the device and open its summary page. Click the Check for Upgrade button to begin the process of upgrading your device.

To set up your device to work with MobileMe, follow these steps:

1. On the Home screen, tap Settings.

2. On the Settings screen, tap Mail, Contacts, Calendars.

3. Check that your Fetch New Data setting is Push. (If it's not, tap Fetch New Data and tap the Push setting so that it reads On, and then return to the Settings screen.)

4. Tap Add Account.

5. On the Add Account screen, tap MobileMe.

6. The MobileMe screen, shown in Figure 9.9, opens. Type in your account information: your name, user name (which is used for your @me.com email address), and password. You can add an optional description, if you want.

7. Tap Next.

8. Turn on each of these settings: Mail, Contacts, Calendars, and Bookmarks (see Figure 9.10).

9. As you turn on settings in step 8, you may see a message asking you to merge your information with MobileMe. If you do, tap the Merge with MobileMe button. This makes sure that you won't get duplicates when you sync your device with MobileMe.

10. Turn on the Find My iPhone (for iPod Touch or iPhone) or Find My iPad feature.

11. Tap Save (on your iPhone) or Done (on your iPad).

Your device syncs with your MobileMe account, bringing your info up-to-date between the device and MobileMe. For example, any Contacts you store in your device are now in the Contacts section of your MobileMe account on www.me.com.

To protect your device in case of loss or theft, set up a passcode lock at the same time you set up your MobileMe account. Tap Settings, General, Passcode Lock. Tap Turn Passcode On, and enter a four-digit passcode (make it something you'll remember). Reenter the passcode to confirm it.

Figure 9.9   *Setting up MobileMe on an iPhone*

Figure 9.10   *Turning on MobileMe services on an iPhone*

 **LET ME TRY IT**

Setting Up MobileMe on a Windows PC

To sync information on your Windows computer and your MobileMe account, start by downloading the latest version of the MobileME Control Panel for Windows (you can download it from http://support.apple.com/downloads/MobileMe_Control_Panel_for_Windows) and installing it on your computer. After you've done that, follow these steps:

1. From the Windows Start menu, open your computer's Control Panel.

2. Select MobileMe.

3. Sign in using your MobileMe user name and password; click Sign In.

4. In the MobileMe Preferences window, click the Sync tab, shown in Figure 9.11.

5. Put a check mark in the Synchronize with MobileMe check box, and then choose your sync preferences:

   - From the drop-down list, select how frequently you want to sync: automatically (the best for keeping your devices up-to-date with each other); manually; or every hour, day, or week.
   - Check the box for the kind of information you want to sync: Contacts, Calendars, and Bookmarks. For each box you check, select the source.
   - If you want to know when a sync is going to change this computer's data, make sure that the Warn When box is checked and select your warning threshold: when any data changes, or when more than 5%, 25%, or 50% changes.

6. Click Sync Now.

Your computer saves your settings and syncs with MobileMe.

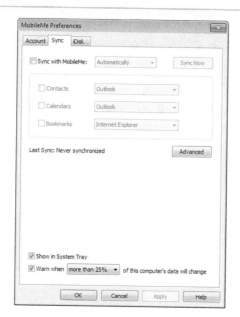

Figure 9.11   *Setting up MobileMe to sync with a Windows PC*

 LET ME TRY IT

Setting Up MobileMe on a Mac

You don't have to install any new software to set up MobileMe with your Mac, but do make sure your software is up-to-date. (From the Apple menu, select Software Update and follow any prompts.) Then set up MobileMe on your computer with these quick steps:

1. From the Apple menu, select System Preferences.

2. Select MobileMe.

3. Sign in using your MobileMe user name and password; click Sign In.

4. Click Sync.

5. Put a check mark in the Synchronize with MobileMe check box, shown in Figure 9.12, and then choose your sync preferences:

   - From the drop-down list, select how frequently you want to sync: automatically (the best for keeping your devices up-to-date with each other); manually; or every hour, day, or week.
   - Check the box for the kind of information you want to sync.

- If you want to know when a sync is going to change this computer's data, make sure that the Warn When box is checked and select your warning threshold: when any data changes, or when more than 5%, 25%, or 50% changes.

6. Click Sync Now.

7. If you own more than one Mac computer, select any other items that you want to sync across all your Macs.

Figure 9.12   *Setting up MobileMe to sync with a Mac*

 LET ME TRY IT

Replacing Data During a Sync

You may find that a sync doesn't overwrite all the cloud-based data (that is, the data stored remotely on Apple's servers) with the latest data from your computer, resulting in duplicates of some items. You can fix this problem with these steps:

1. Open MobileMe via the Control Panel (in Windows) or System Preferences (on a Mac).

2. Select the Sync tab (shown in Figure 9.11 for Windows and Figure 9.12 for Macs).

3. Click the Advanced button.

4. From the Registered Computer list, select the computer you want to sync.

5. Click the Reset Sync Data button.

6. The Reset Sync Data dialog box, shown in Figure 9.13, opens. From the Replace drop-down list, select the kind of data you want to overwrite in the cloud:

   - In Windows, you select All Sync Info, Bookmarks, Calendars, or Contacts.
   - On a Mac, you select All Sync Info, Bookmarks, Calendars, or Contacts. You have other options, such as Mail Accounts, but these don't apply to syncing your iPod Touch, iPhone, or iPad.

7. Select On MobileMe with Sync Info from This Computer. This tells MobileMe to overwrite data in the cloud with data from your computer. The arrows in the dialog box point from the computer icon to the cloud icon, making it clear which way the data will go.

8. Click Replace.

MobileMe replaces the data it's stored in the cloud with data from your computer. You can also sync the other way, if you want to overwrite data on your computer with data you've store on MobileMe. In that case, select On This Computer with Sync Info from MobileMe, making the arrows point from the cloud icon to the computer icon.

Figure 9.13   *Overwriting MobileMe data with data from your computer*

 **LET ME TRY IT**

Setting Up Find My iPhone/iPad

The Find My iPhone/iPad service used to be available only to people who paid $99 a year to subscribe to the full, bells-and-whistles version of MobileMe. Fortunately, Apple recently made this useful service available as a free app in the App Store. So if your device is lost or stolen, you can locate it, lock it, or delete its data.

First, make sure you have a compatible device: a fourth-generation iPod Touch, an iPhone 4, or an iPad running iOS 4.2. (You can upgrade to the latest version of iOS via iTunes—connect your device, select it in the source list, and click the Upgrade button.)

Next, go to the App Store and search for Find My iPhone or Find My iPad. Download and install the app, and then set it up with these quick steps:

1. On your device, tap Settings, and select Mail, Contacts, Calendars.

2. Tap Add Account and select MobileMe.

3. Type in your Apple ID and password. Or, if you're already a MobileMe subscriber, type in the email address and password you use for me.com.

4. Check your email for a verification message from Apple. Click the Verify Now link and sign in with your Apple ID and password.

5. On your device's MobileMe screen, turn on Find My iPhone/iPad.

6. Tap Allow.

Your account is all set up. And it didn't cost you a penny.

Sharing Your iTunes Library

Mom always said, "It's nice to share." With iTunes, sharing is better than nice—it's easy. If you've ever looked for a song in your iTunes library on one computer and then realized that the song is in the library of a different computer, you'll appreciate sharing. It lets you share iTunes libraries among up to five computers that are connected to a network.

When you share your library with other computers connected to the same network, you enable people using those computers to see and play items from your library on their computers. (For this to work, both your computer and the networked computer must be turned on and have iTunes open.) You can share your entire library or just part of it.

Sharing your library as described in this section lets you select and play items from your iTunes library on a networked computer. It doesn't let you import items from your library to other computers.

Ⓖ *To find out how to import items from another iTunes library on the same network, **see** "Home Sharing" (coming up in this chapter).*

 SHOW ME   Media 9.3—Sharing in iTunes
Access this video file through your registered Web Edition at
my.safaribooksonline.com/9780132660273/media.

Setting Up Sharing

To allow other computers on a network to share your iTunes library, select Edit, Preferences (on a PC) or iTunes, Preferences (on a Mac), and click the Sharing tab, shown in Figure 9.14.

Put a check mark in the box labeled Share My Library on My Local Network. When you check that box, iTunes gives you some options:

- **Share Entire Library**—This option gives connected computers the option to browse, select, and play items from your whole iTunes library.

- **Share Selected Playlists**—When you pick this option, iTunes displays a list of your libraries and playlists. Put a check mark next to those you want to share.

- **Require Password**—Maybe you want to have access to your library from networked computers but don't want just anyone rifling through your items. Put a check in this check box and type in a password to restrict access; only someone who knows the password can use your library.

When you get sharing set the way you want it, click OK.

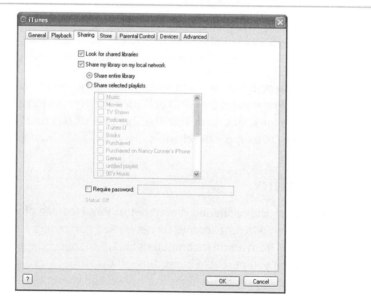

Figure 9.14 *Choosing Sharing settings*

Using Shared Libraries

To find shared libraries on your network, make sure iTunes knows to look for libraries that are being shared. Select Edit, Preferences (on a PC) or iTunes, Preferences (on a Mac), and click the Sharing tab (see Figure 9.14). Make sure there's a check mark in the Look for Shared Libraries check box and click OK.

Shared libraries appear in the left source list under Shared. If necessary, click the triangle beside Shared so that it points downward and expands to show the shared libraries and playlists available. Click a library or playlist to listen to its contents.

If you don't see Shared in the source list (and you're sure that the Look for Shared Libraries check box is turned on), no shared libraries are currently available. Make sure the computer that holds the library you want is turned on, with iTunes open and sharing turned on.

If you close iTunes while someone is using a shared library, you see a warning letting you know that your iTunes library is being shared right now. When you see this warning, you can choose any of these options:

- **Quit**—When you quit iTunes while someone else is using your library, the other person gets kicked out of your library and returned to his or her own library.

- **Don't Quit**—This cancels the close operation so the other person can continue to use your library.

- **Time out**—If you fail to click either Quit or Don't Quit within 20 seconds, iTunes closes anyway, disconnecting any other users from your library.

If you decide you no longer want to share your library, you can turn off sharing. Just select Edit, Preferences (on a PC) or iTunes, Preferences (on a Mac); click Sharing; and remove the check mark from the Share My Library on My Local Network check box. Click OK to apply the change.

Home Sharing

If sharing is good, Home Sharing is even better. Why? Instead of merely being able to play items from different libraries on networked computers, Home Sharing lets you *import* items from another computer's library so that you have a copy on both computers. When you purchase items through the iTunes Store, you can even use Home Sharing to import those items to a networked computer—automatically.

Home Sharing lets you share music files (MP3, Apple Lossless, AIFF, WAV, and AAC formats), movies, and radio station links. You can't share files QuickTime sound files or files you bought from Audible.com.

Getting Started with Home Sharing

Before you can use Home Sharing, you need to turn it on for all the computers that will share their libraries. (You can link up to five computers through Home Sharing.) When you turn on Home Sharing, each participating computer can see, play, and import items from the other Home Sharing–enabled computers.

To use Home Sharing, you need an account with the iTunes Store. Use the same iTunes Store account when you turn on Home Sharing for each computer involved.

ⓖ *To set up an account at the iTunes Store,* **see** *"Creating Your iTunes Store Account"* *(in Chapter 3, "Shopping in the iTunes Store").*

 LET ME TRY IT

Setting Up Home Sharing

To get started with Home Sharing, follow these steps:

1. Select Advanced, Turn On Home Sharing.

2. The Home Sharing page opens, with your Apple ID already filled in (see Figure 9.15). Type in your password and click Create Home Share.

3. iTunes turns on Home Sharing for this computer. Click Done.

4. Repeat steps 1–3 on any other computers you want to include in Home Sharing.

Figure 9.15   *Turning on Home Sharing*

Using Home Sharing

After you've set up Home Sharing on the computers in your home network, you can rummage around other libraries and import items to any of your computers that have Home Sharing turned on. To see another computer's library, both computers must be on and must have iTunes open.

You have several options for importing items to iTunes libraries that participate in your Home Sharing network:

- **Import Individual Items from Another Computer**—Look in the navigation bar under Shared and click the library you want. Select an item or a group of items, drag the selection to your library, and drop it there.

- **Import Everything from a Library on Another Computer**—Click the library you want (under Shared) in the source list. Click the Import button in the lower-right part of the screen (see Figure 9.16). iTunes imports the entire library.

- **Automatically Import Purchases into This Computer's Library**—When new content gets added to a shared library on another computer from the iTunes Store, you can use Home Sharing to automatically import a copy to this computer. Click the library you want (under Shared) to open it. Click the bottom-right Settings button to open the Home Sharing Settings dialog box (shown in Figure 9.16). Put a check mark next to the type of content you want to import, and then click OK.

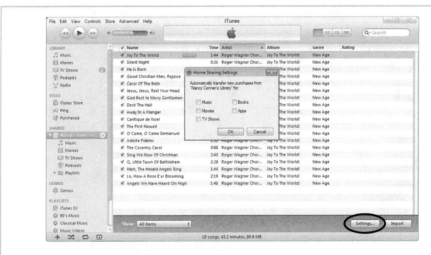

Figure 9.16 *Setting Home Sharing to import new iTunes Store purchases from another library—automatically*

If you decide that you don't want to use Home Sharing, you can turn it off. If you already have five computers using Home Sharing, for example, you might want to turn off Home Sharing on an old computer so you can enable it on a new one. In iTunes, select Advanced, Turn Off Home Sharing. When you turn off Home Sharing, other computers on your home network no longer have access to the library on this computer, and this computer no longer has access to other computers' iTunes libraries. And if you decide that it's nice to share after all, you can turn Home Sharing back on from the Advanced menu, as described earlier in this section.

Playing Music throughout the House with AirPlay

You don't have to hang out in front of your computer or carry your iPod around with you to listen to music throughout the house. Say you have a set of speakers in the living room, another in the kitchen, and another in your bedroom. As you move from room to room, wouldn't it be great to hear your favorite music—without interruption—wherever you are?

In iTunes 10, AirPlay (a new and improved version of AirTunes) lets you stream music to speakers throughout your home. AirPlay works over a wireless or Ethernet connection to play music from iTunes on AirPlay-enabled speakers. Along with the songs, AirPlay streams track information. So if your AirPlay-enabled receiver can show track information, you can see song titles, artists, album names, playing time, and even album artwork, in some cases, at a glance.

To use AirPlay, you need the right hardware: speakers that work with AirPlay technology. At this writing, these manufacturers make AirPlay-enabled receivers and speakers:

- Bowers & Wilkins
- Denon
- iHome
- JBL
- Marantz

More manufacturers will most likely come on board, so check with your favorite brand to see if their products work with AirPlay.

TELL ME MORE   Media 9.4—AirPlay and AirTunes

Access this audio recording through your registered Web Edition at
my.safaribooksonline.com/9780132660273/media.

Another option for streaming your iTunes content is through Apple TV. **See** *"Apple TV and iTunes" (in Chapter 6) for more information.*

Setting Up AirPlay

To start using AirPlay, make sure that your AirPlay-enabled receiver and speakers are connected to the same network as the computer that holds your iTunes library.

Open iTunes and select Edit, Preferences (on a PC) or iTunes, Preferences (on a Mac). Select Devices. On the Devices tab, shown in Figure 9.17, make sure there's a check mark in the check box labeled Look for Remote Speakers Connected with AirPlay. If you want to be able to control iTunes from your AirPlay-enabled device, check the box labeled Allow iTunes Control from Remote Speakers. Click OK.

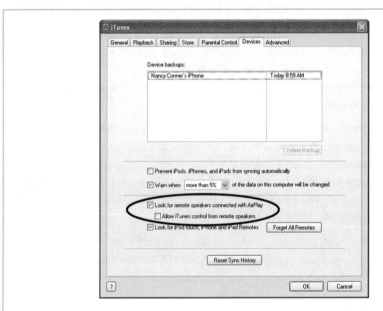

Figure 9.17   *Telling iTunes to look for AirPlay-enabled speakers*

When iTunes detects AirPlay-enabled speakers, a Multiple Speakers button appears in the lower-right part of the iTunes screen. Click Multiple Speakers and select the speakers you want to stream music to.

The number of speakers you can stream to depends on several factors, such as how much traffic is on your network right now and the distance between the computer running iTunes and the set of speakers. Typically, you can expect to stream to three to six sets of speakers.

You can also control volume remotely from the Multiple Speakers window or by using the main volume control in the upper-left corner of the iTunes window. Move the slider to adjust the relative volume of the AirPlay-connected speakers.

Ⓖ *Use the Remote app to control iTunes remotely from anywhere in your house.* ***See*** *"Controlling iTunes Remotely" (in Chapter 11, "iTunes Tips and Tricks").*

If you like talking music with your friends, you'll love Ping, a social network that's new in iTunes 10. Discover new music, share your favorites, and follow your friends and favorite artists.

10

Ping: iTunes Goes Social

iTunes 10 brings a whole new world of music-based social networking to iTunes. It's called Ping, and it's a great way to connect with friends, your favorite artists, and fellow music lovers. When you turn on Ping, you can connect with other iTunes users who share your interests and see what they're listening to. When you buy, like, or review music in the iTunes Store, the activity appears in your Ping Recent Activity feed, where anyone who follows you learns about it. In the same way, you're informed of the purchases, reviews, and other activities of the people you follow.

In this chapter, you'll learn how to get started with Ping: create your profile, choose your privacy settings, and find people and artists to follow. A quick guided tour gets you familiar with the site and shows you how to use Ping with the iTunes sidebar so that you know what's going on even when you're not in the iTunes Store. Other topics covered include inviting your friends to join Ping, interacting with other users, finding concerts near you (as well as getting tickets and letting your friends know you'll be there), reviewing albums, and using Ping on your iPod Touch, iPhone, or iPad.

The fun is all in the interaction, so let's get started.

Getting Started with Ping

Ping is part of the iTunes Store, so you need an iTunes Store account to use it. After you have your account in place, it's easy to turn on Ping and create your profile.

⊙ *Don't have an iTunes Store account yet?* **See** *"Creating Your iTunes Store Account" (in Chapter 3, "Shopping in the iTunes Store") to learn how to set one up.*

Creating a Ping Profile

Every Ping user has a profile that contains (at the very least) his or her name. But to get the most out of Ping, you should create a profile that shares your musical tastes and makes it easy for friends and like-minded music fans to find you.

 LET ME TRY IT

Turning on Ping and Creating Your Profile

To get started with Ping, follow these steps:

1. In the left iTunes source list, under Store, click Ping. (Alternatively, open the iTunes sidebar by clicking the button at the status bar's right side; click Learn More.)

2. Click Turn On Ping.

3. Sign in to your iTunes Store account using your Apple ID and password.

4. Create your profile; see Figure 10.1 for the first step. Your profile holds public information that's visible to other Ping users:

   - **Name**—iTunes has already filled in the First Name and Last Name fields, based on your iTunes Store account. You must use the same name for Ping that you use for your iTunes Store account—no nicknames allowed.
   - **Gender**—Choose yours from the drop-down list.
   - **Photo**—Click the Add Photo button to find and select a picture from your computer to upload to Ping. Ping shows you the uploaded photo in an Edit Photo dialog box so that you can adjust its size or choose a different photo. When the picture looks good, click Set.
   - **Where I Live**—This field is already filled in, based on the information in your iTunes Store account.
   - **About Me**—Write a brief description of yourself in this text box.
   - **Genres I Like**—Check up to three genres that best describe your favorite kinds of music.

   To create a profile, the First Name, Last Name, and Gender fields are required. All others are optional.

5. Click Continue.

Figure 10.1 *Creating a Ping profile: giving your information*

6. On the next page, shown in Figure 10.2, tell Ping how to display music that you like—up to ten selections—on your profile. Choose one of these options:

   - **Automatically Display All Music I Like, Rate, or Purchase**—When you choose this option, your profile automatically reflects your favorite music: Music that you buy, rate, or give a "Like" thumbs-up shows on your profile.
   - **Manually Pick the Music to Display**—This option puts you in control of the music that shows on your profile; you pick your favorite songs to display there. When you select this option, a search box appears (see Figure 10.2) that lets you search your iTunes library for the tunes you want to show on your profile.
   - **Don't Display Music That I Like on My Profile**—If you prefer to keep your musical tastes to yourself, choose this option.

7. Click Continue.

8. Choose your Ping privacy settings (see Figure 10.3):

   - **Allow People to Follow Me**—If you want your friends to find you and see what you're doing, select this option.
   - **Require Approval to Follow Me**—When you allow people to follow you, you can choose to have Ping check with you before it approves any follower. When you select the box that turns on this option, Ping sends you a notification when someone wants to follow you, and you can approve or deny that person.

- **Don't Allow People to Follow Me**—When you choose this option, you can follow other people, but no one can follow you.

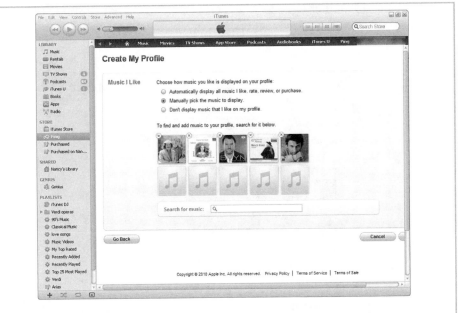

Figure 10.2   *Creating a Ping profile: selecting music to display on your profile*

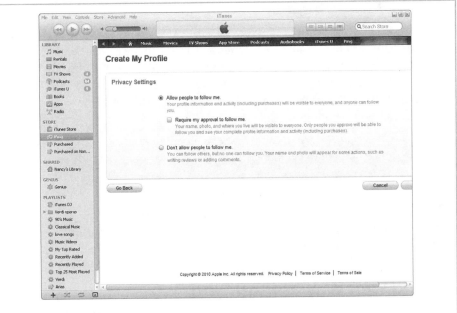

Figure 10.3   *Creating a Ping profile: choosing privacy settings*

9. Click Done to create your profile and start using Ping.

After your account is set up, iTunes opens Ping (see Figure 10.4) and sends a welcome email to your registered email address. (You don't have to respond to the email—your account is already set up.)

Figure 10.4   *The Ping home page*

If you're a musician, you must have content available in the iTunes Store before you can create an artist's profile in Ping. If you've signed with a record label, contact your iTunes label representative to learn how to set up your profile. You can learn more about iTunes requirements for setting up artist profiles at www. apple.com/itunes/content-providers.

If you're a musician and you don't yet have a record deal, you can create a regular Ping profile and tell the world about your music in your About Me section.

TELL ME MORE   Media 10.1—Ping and Privacy
Access this audio recording through your registered Web Edition at
my.safaribooksonline.com/9780132660273/media.

Finding Your Way around Ping

After you've turned on Ping and created your profile, Ping looks something like the page shown in Figure 10.4. Here's what you'll find there:

- **Ping links**—On the right side of the page are these links (they may change a bit, depending on which page you're on):
  - **My Profile**—This link takes you to your profile page, where you can see your profile as it looks to others and edit your information.
  - **My Reviews**—When you've reviewed at least one album, song, or video, this link opens your reviews.
  - **People**—Click this link to view and manage the people you follow and those who follow you.
  - **Featured Artists**—This link takes you to a page where you can read about and follow artists who are active on Ping.
  - **Featured People**—Artists aren't the only people on Ping. This page highlights celebrities, songwriters, music industry professionals, and just plain interesting music lovers who have a following on Ping.

Click any name or photo on the Featured Artists or Featured People page to see that person's profile.

- **Search box**—This box lets you search Ping for a specific artist or friend so you can connect.

- **Invite button**—Click this button to begin the process of inviting your friends to join Ping.

- **Artists We Recommend You Follow**—This list is ranked by popularity (total number of followers), not your particular musical tastes. So if you listen only to jazz, don't be surprised to see Lady Gaga or Taylor Swift showing up here.

- **Recent Activity**—This newsfeed in this section shows what the friends and artists you follow have been doing on Ping lately.

To make your Ping home page less cluttered, point at the Search for People or Artists section and/or the Artists We Recommend Your Follow section, and click the x that appears in the upper-left corner. The section you closed moves to the right side of the page, leaving more room for your Recent Activity feed.

 SHOW ME   Media 10.2—Taking a Look around Ping
Access this video file through your registered Web Edition at
my.safaribooksonline.com/9780132660273/media.

Following Artists and Friends

In Ping, all the fun comes from following interesting people: artists, celebrities, friends, and people who love the same kind of music you do. You have lots of options for finding and following people on Ping.

 SHOW ME   Media 10.3—Finding and Following People
Access this video file through your registered Web Edition at
my.safaribooksonline.com/9780132660273/media.

Following Featured Artists and People

iTunes lists some of the most popular artists and people who are active on Ping on its Featured Artists and Featured People pages. You can get to either of these pages from the Ping links on the right side of the Ping home page (see Figure 10.4) and most other pages in Ping. Figure 10.5 shows an example of the Featured People page. When you find someone you want to follow, click that person's Follow button.

Figure 10.5   *The Featured People page*

If you want to check out someone's profile before you decide whether to follow, click that person's name or photo. This opens the person's profile (like the one shown in Figure 10.6), where you can see recent activity, preferred music, reviews, other followers, and more. To follow someone from a profile, click the Follow button.

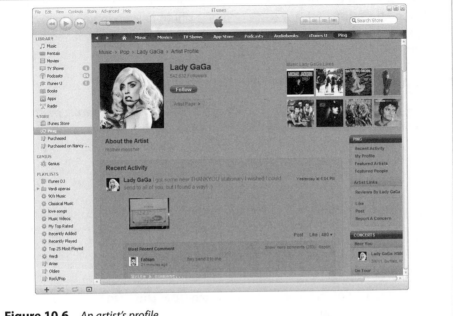

Figure 10.6   *An artist's profile*

Viewing Artist Pages in the iTunes Store

In Ping, an artist's profile offers information about the artist—favorite music, recent activity on the site, upcoming concerts, and so on (a lot like your own profile). Each artist's profile also has a link to that artist's page in the iTunes Store. An Artist Page lists all of that artist's albums, songs, and music videos available for purchase through the iTunes Store. You can preview songs, go to an item's page, or buy items right from the Artist Page.

In Ping, you can get to an artist's Artist Page in either of these ways:

- **From the Featured Artists list**—Click the Artist Page link to the right of an artist's name.

- **From an artist's profile**—Click the Artist Page button below the artist's name.

 To find out how to buy items in the iTunes Store, **see** "Buying Music and Other Media" (in Chapter 3).

Finding People with Similar Tastes

When you follow a favorite artist, you can see who else is following that artist and check out those followers' profiles—maybe you'll find someone interesting to follow that way. On the right side of each artist's profile is a section called People, listing some of the artist's followers. Click See All to view a list of everyone who's following the artist. Click any name or profile photo to learn more about a follower (depending on that person's privacy settings). If the person looks like someone you would enjoy following, click Follow.

Searching for a Specific Person

Instead of browsing for people to follow, you can search for a specific person— your favorite artist, for example, or a friend who's on Ping. At the top of the Ping home page, type the name of the person you're searching for into the Search box and press Enter.

> You can also search for other Ping users from your People page. Under Ping links, click People, and then use the Search box in the Find People section at the right.

Ping returns a list of matches (and near-matches), as shown in Figure 10.7. Results are split into Artists and People—regular Ping users who don't have an artist's account. (If you get a lot of results and want to look only for artists, click the upper-right Artists link.) Click Follow to become a follower of any person on the page, or click a name or photo to see that person's profile.

Figure 10.7 *A search results page, where you can see all results or limit results to just artists by clicking one of the circled links*

Inviting Friends to Join Ping

If you can't find a friend on Ping, you can nudge that friend to join by sending an email invitation. On the Ping home page, click Invite. This opens a dialog box similar to the one shown in Figure 10.8. Type in your friend's email address (if you want to send multiple invitations, separate email addresses with commas or spaces) and, if you want, add an optional message. Click Invite.

iTunes sends an email to the addresses you listed, inviting your friends to join Ping. The email comes from the iTunes Store and has your name in the subject line: "Jane Smith has invited you to join iTunes Ping." The email explains what Ping is and includes two links:

- A link to the iTunes download page, for people who don't yet have iTunes

- A link that opens Ping in iTunes, for people who have iTunes but haven't yet turned on Ping

Figure 10.8   *Sending an invitation to join Ping; click the Invite button (circled) to open the invitation dialog box.*

If you use Twitter, you can connect Ping with your Twitter account and share your Ping likes and activities. Under Find People, select Connect to Twitter. Type your Twitter user name (or the email address you use for your Twitter account) and your Twitter password. Click Sign In—and your Ping and Twitter accounts are connected!

Finding Concerts

Listening to recorded music through iTunes at home or on your iPod is great, but most music lovers agree that nothing beats the energy, excitement, and sound of a live performance. Use Ping to find out when your favorite artists are on tour—you can even buy tickets and let your friends know you'll be there.

To look for concerts, go to any artist's profile. On the right side of the page, look for a Concerts section. If the artist is currently touring, you'll see upcoming dates and venues in that section. (If one of those concerts is near you, it appears at the top of the list.) Click See All for a full list on the artist's Tour Info page, shown in Figure 10.9.

On the Tour Info page, click Tickets to open a third-party ticket site (such as Ticketmaster) in a new window, where you can purchase tickets. Click I'm Going to inform your followers that you'll be at this concert. When you do, a dialog box opens so you can add an optional comment about the event; type in a comment if you want (like "Let's meet up in the lobby!"), and then click Post to put the comment in your Recent Activity feed.

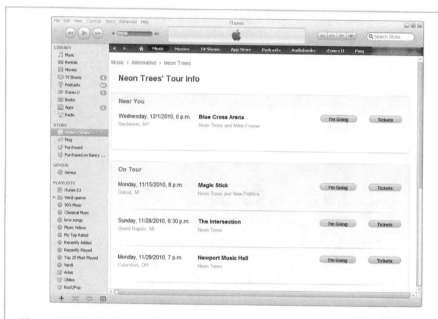

Figure 10.9   *An artist's Tour Info page*

Ping lists only concerts whose tickets are available online through a third-party ticket site. At this writing, those sites include Ticketmaster.com, LiveNation.com, and TicketWeb.com. You won't find concerts at venues where tickets are available only at the door—to learn about those concerts, check out the artist's website.

Using the iTunes Sidebar

You can keep tabs on your favorite artists and friends even when you don't have Ping open. The iTunes sidebar, shown in Figure 10.10, keeps you in touch with your Recent Activity feed while you do other things in iTunes, such as browse your Music library or edit a playlist. But the iTunes sidebar is more than just Ping. It combines Ping activity with Genius recommendations—music you might want to know about based on your library and listening habits.

> The iTunes sidebar displays only as you work with your Music library or your playlists. It doesn't show if you're in other parts of your iTunes library, such as movies or books.

To open the iTunes sidebar, click the Show/Hide iTunes sidebar button (circled in Figure 10.10) at the status bar's far right. The sidebar opens, displaying the currently selected track at the top, with convenient buttons that let you Like or Post the track to your Recent Activity feed. So when a track plays and you think, "Hey, I really like this song," you can immediately share your enthusiasm with your Ping followers.

Figure 10.10   *The iTunes sidebar, showing Ping activity*

Beneath the current track is your Recent Activity feed, showing the most recent posts. If you want to see more of this feed, click the See All link above the feed to go to Ping and read all of your posts.

You can decide what you want your iTunes sidebar to display: just Ping information, just Genius recommendations, or both. To set up your sidebar the way you want it, select Edit, Preferences (in Windows) or iTunes, Preferences (on a Mac). On the General tab, put a check mark in the Ping and Genius boxes if you want both of these in your sidebar. If you want to remove Ping or Genius from the sidebar, make sure there's no check mark in the associated box. Click OK to save your settings.

Getting Social on Ping

Now that you're following some artists and other people on Ping—and maybe have picked up a few followers of your own—you're ready to get the most out of Ping. Interact with others, manage followers, share your favorite music, and manage your activities—this section shows you how.

Interacting with Others

After you've started following some people, their recent activity—posts, songs or albums they've liked or bought, reviews they've written, people they've followed, and so on—appears in your Recent Activity feed (see Figure 10.11 for an example). This is the same page that welcomes you when you open Ping, and you can always find it by clicking Recent Activity in the Ping links on the right.

You can interact with the people you follow by responding to their activity in any of these ways:

- **Like an activity**—Click the Like button to the right of an activity to show your approval.

- **Comment on an activity**—Beneath each activity is a text box where you can write a comment about the post. Type in your comment and click the Post Comment button to share your thoughts.

- **Read others' comments**—The most recent comment appears below each activity. If you want to read more comments, click the Show More Comments link on the right.

- **Post an activity to your followers**—Click the Post link to share an activity with your own followers. When you click this link, the activity appears on your profile and in the Recent Activity feed of anyone who follows you.

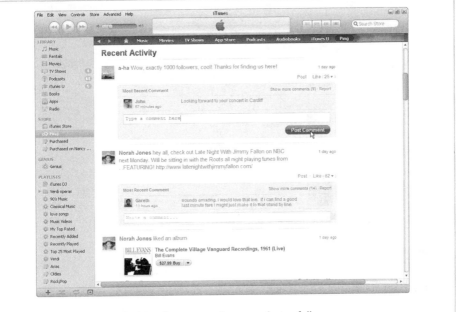

Figure 10.11 *Recent Activity shows posts from people you follow.*

Managing Friends and Followers

After you've followed some people and gained some followers yourself, you can manage your Ping relationship on the People page (see Figure 10.12). To get there, click People in your Ping links on the right.

As Figure 10.12 shows, your People page has two tabs: one listing people you follow and the other listing people who follow you. People are added to these lists in chronological order, with the most recent additions at the top of the list. You can sort the list by alphabetical order (ascending or descending) by selecting the option you want from the upper-right Sort By drop-down list.

Figure 10.12   *A People page, which shows people and artists you follow*

Handling Follow Requests

If you've set your privacy settings to require your approval before someone can follow you, you need to manage any follow requests that you get. With this setting, when another Ping member clicks the Follow button on your profile, iTunes emails you a notification that someone wants to follow you. You'll also see a Follow Requests link in your Ping links, followed by a number that shows how many requests you have.

🄖 *For more about Ping's privacy settings, listen to "Ping and Privacy" (mentioned earlier in this chapter).*

When you receive a request from someone who wants to follow you, you can handle it in one of these ways:

- Click the link in your notification email that reads, "To confirm or ignore this request, click here."

- In Ping, click the Follow Requests link in your Ping links section on the right.

- In Ping, click People under Ping links and make sure the Follow Requests tab is selected.

Any of these routes takes you to the Follow Requests tab of your People page, shown in Figure 10.13. This tab shows who's requesting to follow you. You can click a person's name or photo to see that person's profile page and learn more about him or her. Click Confirm to allow the person to start following you, or click Ignore to deny the request.

After you confirm a follow request, Ping immediately gives you the option to follow the person back. Click Follow if you want to do so.

Figure 10.13 *Handling a follow request*

Reporting Inappropriate Behavior

If you see someone behaving in a way that doesn't respect the Ping community—such as posting spam comments or hate speech—you can report that bad behavior. If you notice an inappropriate post or comment in your Recent Activity feed, you can report the problem then and there. Above and to the right of the problematic post, click the Report link. This opens the Report a Concern dialog box, shown in Figure 10.14.

Choose your concern from the drop-down list: You can report offensive comments, inappropriate photos or videos, spam, or any other action that you feel is inappropriate. Optionally, you can add a comment in the Comments box. When you've expressed your concern, click Submit.

Reporting a concern can get the offending action removed or, in some cases, ban a user from Ping.

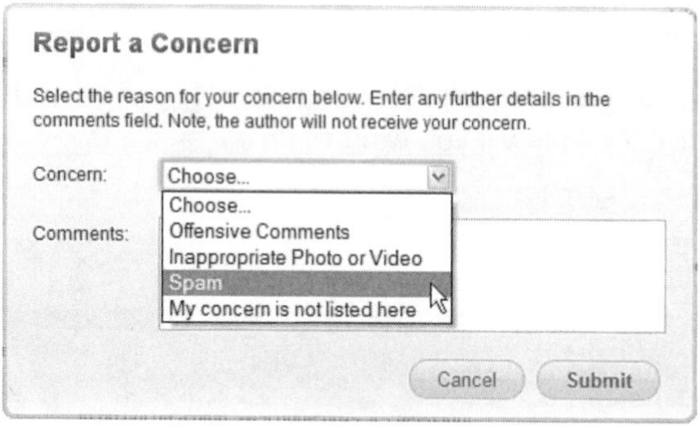

Report a Concern

Select the reason for your concern below. Enter any further details in the comments field. Note, the author will not receive your concern.

Concern: Choose...

> Choose...
> Offensive Comments
> Inappropriate Photo or Video
> Spam
> My concern is not listed here

Comments:

Cancel   Submit

Figure 10.14   *Reporting inappropriate behavior*

You can also report inappropriate behavior from any user's profile page. In the Ping links on the right, click Report a Concern to open the dialog box shown in Figure 10.14.

Unfollowing Someone

Tastes change, and maybe that band that seemed so cutting-edge a year ago no longer thrills you. If you no longer want to follow someone, you can remove him or her from the list of people you follow from either of these places:

- **Your People page**—Click the People I Follow tab and find the person you want to stop following. Click the Stop Following button below the person's name.

- **The person's profile**—If you're on the profile page of the person you no longer want to follow, look in the Ping links on the right. Click Stop Following.

When you stop following someone, iTunes removes that person from your People I Follow list and the person's posts disappear from your Recent Activity feed.

Sharing Music with Your Followers

Love a song? Hate it? Let the world know! Ping gives you several ways to share music—and your thoughts about it—with your followers. Here's a quick break-down:

- **Liking a song or album**—When you click the Like button for some music, you give it a quick thumbs-up so your followers know you enjoyed it.

- **Posting a song or album**—You highlight the song or album, along with a comment about it, in your Recent Activity feed.

- **Rating an album**—When you rate an album, you give it a grade, from a low of one star to a high of five stars.

- **Reviewing an album**—When you want to share your opinion about an album at length, this is the best way to do it. Reviews get posted on the album's page in the iTunes Store and in your Recent Activity feed.

This section covers all the different ways you can share music on Ping.

 SHOW ME   Media 10.4—Sharing Music on Ping
Access this video file through your registered Web Edition at
my.safaribooksonline.com/9780132660273/media.

 LET ME TRY IT

Liking or Posting a Song from Your Music Library

When you come across music from your iTunes library that you want to share, here's what to do:

1. In your iTunes Music library, use List or Album List view to find the song you want to share. Select the song.

2. Click the Ping button that appears to the right of the selected song title.

3a. If you want to tell others that you like the song, choose Like from the context menu.

3b. If you want to post the song in Ping, choose Post from the context menu.

3c. Choosing Post opens the Post As dialog box, shown in Figure 10.15. Type in a comment about the song (telling your followers why you like it, for example). Click Post.

4. iTunes posts the song (along with your comment if you chose Post) to your Ping profile. It also appears in the Recent Activity posts of anyone who follows you.

When you share a song in Ping, your friends and followers can listen to a sample of the song right from your post by clicking its Play button. If they like what they hear, they can click the song's Buy button and buy it then and there. Or they can click the song to go to its album in the iTunes Store.

Figure 10.15 *Posting a song from your Music library to Ping*

Liking or Posting a Song from the iTunes Store

When you're browsing the iTunes Store and come across a great song, you can share your find with your friends on Ping. Next to the song's Buy button (at the far right of the listing) is a downward-pointing arrow; click that. From the context menu that appears, choose either Like or Post. (If you choose Post, type in a comment and then click the Post button.) iTunes lets all your Ping friends know about the great song on your profile and in the Recent Activity section of your followers.

ⓖ *For tips on finding music in the iTunes Store,* ***see*** *"Browsing for Music" and "Searching for Music and Other Content" (both in Chapter 3).*

 LET ME TRY IT

Liking or Posting an Album from Your Music Library

To share an album from your iTunes Music library, follow these steps:

1. In your iTunes Music library, click the Grid View button (at the top of the screen) to display your library in Grid view.

2. Find the album you want to share on Ping and either right-click it (on a PC) or Ctrl-click it (on a Mac).

3a. If you want to tell others that you like the album, choose Like from the context menu.

3b. If you want to post the album in Ping, choose Post from the context menu.

3c. Choosing Post opens the Post As dialog box, which looks just like the one shown for a song (see Figure 10.15). Type an optional comment about the album. Click Post.

4. iTunes posts the album (along with your comment, if you chose Post) to your Ping profile. It also appears in the Recent Activity feed of anyone who follows you.

Liking or Posting an Album from the iTunes Store

Just as you can like or post any song from the iTunes Store, you can do the same with an album. Open the album's page in the iTunes Store. On the left side, below the information about the album, are Like and Post buttons for the album, as shown in Figure 10.16. Click the one you want (if you're posting the album, enter an optional comment in the Post As dialog box).

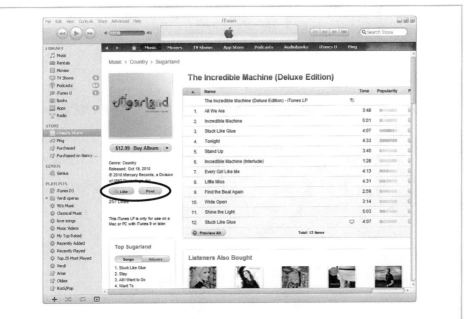

Figure 10.16 *Liking or posting an album from its iTunes Store page*

When you click an album's Like button on its iTunes Store page, iTunes records your vote. Look below the Like button to see how many people have clicked the button to show they like the album.

LET ME TRY IT

Rating and Reviewing an Album

When you review an album in the iTunes Store, you share your opinion with iTunes Store shoppers and your followers on Ping, both at the same time. Reviews get posted on the album's page in the iTunes Store and linked to via the My Reviews link on your Ping profile. You can just rate an album (assign it the number of stars you think it deserves), or you can write a full review to share your thoughts in more detail.

Here's how to rate and review an album in iTunes:

1. In the iTunes Store, go to the page of the album you want to review.

2. In the Customer Reviews section (just below the Customer Reviews heading), click the Write a Review link.

3. If prompted, sign in to your iTunes Store account.

4. In the Write a Review form (see Figure 10.17), click the number of stars you want to assign to the album: one star means you hated it, five stars means you think it's great.

Figure 10.17   *Reviewing an album*

5. Give your review a title (optional) in the Title box. This could be something like "My favorite album ever!" or "I wish this band would go back to its roots."

6. Type your review (optional) into the Review text box. A review can be up to 6,000 characters, including spaces.

The average iTunes album review is about 200 characters.

7. When your review looks good (take the time to read it through for typos), click Submit.

Managing Your Ping Activities

As you spend time on Ping, you may want to change your profile or delete a post or comment you made. Read on to find out how.

Editing Your Profile

Maybe you've discovered a great new album that you want to list as one of your favorites. Maybe you want a new profile picture. Or maybe you've moved to a different town. When you want to make changes to your Ping profile, start on your profile page. (In your Ping links, click My Profile.) When your profile opens, click Edit Profile.

The Edit My Profile page opens. This looks exactly like the form you filled out to create your profile, except that your current information is already filled in. Make whatever changes you want: photo, town, About Me description, favorite genres and albums, or privacy settings. When you're finished, click Save to apply the changes to your profile.

You can't change one piece of information in your Ping profile, and that's your name. Because Ping is tied to your iTunes Store account, it uses the same information you submitted to set up your account in the iTunes Store. Ping doesn't allow nicknames or pseudonyms—the name you use to shop is the name you use to socialize.

Deleting a Post

If you post about something and then change your mind and want to take it back, it's easy to delete a post. Go to your profile and, in your Recent Activity feed, find the post you want to delete. Click the Remove link on its right side to remove the post.

Deleting a Comment

You can remove comments you make on others' posts. Use either of these methods:

- In your Recent Activity feed or on the profile page of the artist or person whose post you commented on, find your comment. When you point at the comment with your mouse pointer, an *x* appears to its right. Click the *x* to delete the comment.

- On your profile, a Remove link appears to the right of each of your comments and posts. Click Remove, and the comment disappears.

> You can also delete any comments that other Ping users make on your posts.

Going Mobile with Ping

You can take Ping with you wherever you go, thanks to your iPod Touch, iPhone, or iPad. Just like on your computer, you'll find Ping in the iTunes Store on your portable device. Tap iTunes and then, at the bottom of the screen, tap Ping. Figure 10.18 shows how Ping looks on an iPhone.

Figure 10.18 *Ping on an iPhone*

Across the top of the screen are three buttons:

- **Activity**—Tap this button to see your Recent Activity feed. Tap any post to read it in full or see the poster's profile. You can also use the Like and Comments buttons to respond to the posts in the feed.

- **People**—Tap this button to see lists of people you follow and people who follow you.

- **My Profile**—View your own Recent Activity by tapping this button. On the page that opens, tap My Info to view your profile.

> You can't edit your Ping profile from your portable device; you have to do that from your computer.

Turning Off Ping

If you decide that Ping isn't for you, you can turn it off from your iTunes Store account. When you turn off Ping, iTunes removes your profile, comments, and Recent Activity list from Ping immediately, but the information hangs around on Apple's servers for a week. So if you change your mind and turn on Ping again, your information is still there. If you don't come back after seven days, though, iTunes permanently deletes your profile information.

 LET ME TRY IT

Turn Off Ping

To turn off Ping and remove your profile information, follow these steps:

1. In iTunes, click iTunes Store in the source list.

2. In the iTunes Store, click your email address at the upper-right to open your account.

3. Type in the password for your iTunes Store account and click View Account.

4. In the Ping section of your account page, click the Turn Off button.

5. If you're sure that you want to stop using Ping, click Turn Off again to confirm.

Get more out of iTunes with the tips and tricks listed in this chapter. From tweaks to trouble-shooting, you'll find ways to optimize your iTunes experience.

11

iTunes Tips and Tricks

If you've read the preceding chapters of this book, you've mastered the basics—and beyond—of iTunes. This chapter supplements your iTunes knowledge with tweaks, fixes, and suggestions to help you get even more out of iTunes.

Whether you want to add lyrics to a song, adjust the length of a track, or listen in a smaller player, you'll find instructions here. You'll also learn how to do things you may not even have realized you could do with iTunes: share files between your computer and your portable device and control iTunes remotely using your iPod Touch, iPhone, or iPad. There's a comprehensive list of keyboard shortcuts for both Windows and Mac users. And if you're having trouble getting iTunes to work properly, check out the list of troubleshooting tips that ends the chapter.

Adding Lyrics to a Song

Some people like to listen to music; others need to know each and every word that's being sung. Whether you like to sing along or just follow along, you can add lyrics to any song in your iTunes library.

First, get the lyrics. You might find these on a band's website or in the booklet that comes with a CD. Next, go to iTunes and select the song you're adding lyrics to. Select File, Get Info and click the Lyrics tab. The Lyrics tab consists of a big text box where you can paste or type in the lyrics you're adding to the song. When you've added the lyrics, click OK to save them.

To view or edit a song's lyrics, repeat the process: Select the song you want; then select File, Get Info and click Lyrics. The lyrics appear in the text box on that tab. You can simply read them or make changes to them. Click OK when you're done.

Using the iTunes Mini Player

When you open iTunes, you see the familiar window that takes up the full screen (or a big portion of it). If you're doing other work on your computer as you listen to music, you have to switch back to the iTunes window when you want to adjust volume, pause playback, see the name of what's playing, or move to another song. Jumping back and forth between the window where you're working and the iTunes window can be distracting.

Enter the iTunes Mini Player, shown in Figure 11.1, which shrinks iTunes to its most basic function: playing music. When you turn on the Mini Player, you can see the name of the current track and control playback without having to look in the full-size iTunes window.

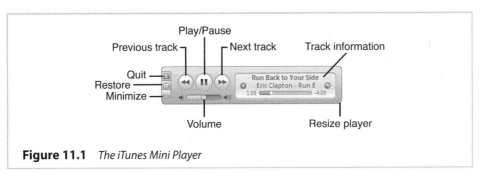

Figure 11.1   *The iTunes Mini Player*

 SHOW ME   Media 11.1—Playing Music with the iTunes Mini Player
Access this video file through your registered Web Edition at
my.safaribooksonline.com/9780132660273/media.

When you want to use the Mini Player, start playing a track, album, or playlist and select View, Switch to Mini Player. (You can also press Ctrl+M on a PC or Cmd-M on a Mac.) As your music plays, you can use the Mini Player to do these actions:

- **Start or pause play**—The familiar Play/Pause button works just as it does in your iTunes Controls.

- **Repeat previous track**—Click the button with the left-pointing arrows to play the previous track again.

- **Jump to next track**—Click the button with the right-pointing arrows to skip ahead to the next track on your list.

- **Adjust the volume**—Move the slider left or right to decrease or increase the volume.

- **View or hide track information**—The Mini Player comes in two sizes. The expanded version (see Figure 11.1) shows track information for the song that's playing. The compact version hides track information, showing just the playback controls. To expand the Mini Player and see track info, point at the player's lower-right corner, click, and drag to the right. To use the compact version and hide track info, point at the lower-right corner, click, and drag to the left.

- **Return to the full-size iTunes window**—On the Mini Player's left side, click the Restore button. You can also return to the full iTunes window by pressing Ctrl+M (on a PC) or Cmd-M (on a Mac).

- **Minimize iTunes**—When you click the left Minimize button, the Mini Player minimizes but keeps playing.

- **Close iTunes**—Click the upper-left *x* to quit iTunes. If you close iTunes this way, the next time you start it again, the Mini Player opens.

You can keep the Mini Player visible, no matter what else you're doing on your computer. In iTunes, select Edit, Preferences (in Windows) or iTunes, Preferences (on a Mac). Click the Advanced tab. Put a check mark in the box labeled Keep Mini Player on Top of All Other Windows. Click OK. Now when you use the Mini Player, it will float over any other windows open on your screen.

Using the iTunes Desktop Player

If your preferences land you somewhere between the Mini Player's minimalism and the full-blown iTunes window's complexity, you'll be pleased to know that there's a middle ground: the iTunes Desktop Player. This controller displays album art along with playback controls, as shown in Figure 11.2.

 SHOW ME   Media 11.2—Playing Music with the iTunes Desktop Player
Access this video file through your registered Web Edition at
my.safaribooksonline.com/9780132660273/media.

To display the Desktop Player, start by playing a song. Make sure that the album cover of the currently playing selection shows in the artwork viewer, in the lower left. (If the artwork viewer is closed, click the upward-pointing triangle just below where it should appear.) Point at the artwork that appears in the artwork viewer.

When the mouse pointer changes to a pointing hand, click the artwork. iTunes launches the Desktop Player in a separate window.

At the top of the player, the title bar shows you what's playing now. In the upper right, you'll find buttons to minimize, restore, and close the player. (Clicking the upper-right x closes the player but leaves iTunes open.) Use the playback controls at the bottom of the player just as you would in iTunes. To make the player the perfect size, click and drag the lower-right resizing handle.

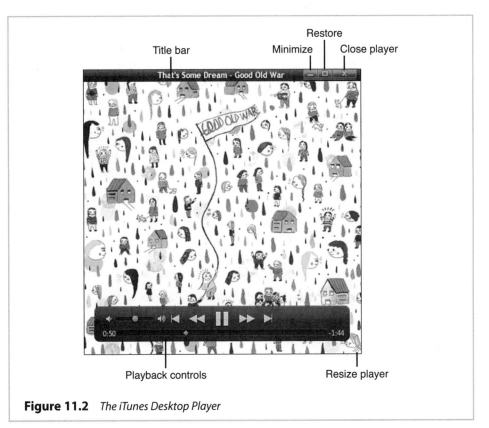

Figure 11.2   *The iTunes Desktop Player*

Controlling iTunes Remotely

You don't have to be tied to your computer to control iTunes. Thanks to Remote, a free app available through Apple's App Store, you can select songs, albums, or playlists to play; choose videos or TV shows to watch; pause playback; adjust the volume; skip to a different track; create playlists; and more—all by using your iPhone Touch, iPhone, or iPad over your home's wireless network. The Remote app is especially useful if you use Apple TV or AirPlay to experience your iTunes library on your TV or remote speakers.

ⓖ *To learn more about Apple TV, **see** "Apple TV and iTunes" (in Chapter 6, "Viewing in iTunes: TV, Movies, and More"). To read about AirPlay, **see** "Playing Music throughout the House with AirPlay" (in Chapter 9, "Syncing and Sharing").*

Getting Started with the Remote App

To use the Remote app, you need to have an iPad, iPod Touch, or iPhone with iOS 3.1.2 or later. To find out which version of iOS you have, go to your device's Home screen; tap Settings, General, About; and look under Version.

ⓖ *When you're using the iTunes DJ to play a live mix, the Remote app lets you— and your guests—request a song remotely. **See** "Requesting a Song Remotely" (in Chapter 5, "Playing with Playlists") for details.*

 LET ME TRY IT

Setting Up the Remote App on Your Portable Device

Begin by downloading the Remote app from the App Store to your device. After you've done that, follow these steps:

1. On your device's Home screen, tap the Remote icon to open the app.

2. Tap Settings.

3. On the Settings screen, shown in Figure 11.3, tap Add an iTunes Library.

4. The app gives you a four-digit passcode. Make a note of it.

5. Open the iTunes library you want to add and, under Devices in the Source list, select your device (it has the Remote icon beside it, as you can see in Figure 11.4).

6. iTunes opens the Add Remote screen, shown in Figure 11.4. Type the four-digit passcode from your device into the boxes.

7. iTunes enables remote access to your library, and your library gets added to the Remote app on your device. Libraries to which you have access appear at the top of the Settings screen, as in Figure 11.3, with a check mark beside the current library.

You're all set to start using Remote (read on to find out how to do that). If you want to add another library, repeat the steps in this list.

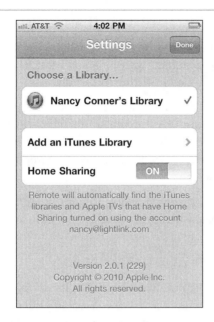

Figure 11.3 *Choosing or adding an iTunes library*

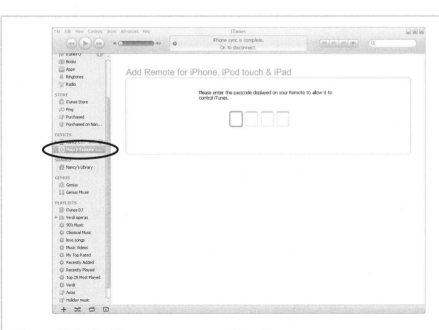

Figure 11.4 *Enabling remote access to an iTunes library*

Turning On Home Sharing in the Remote App

If you've enabled Home Sharing on computers linked by a network, you can turn on Home Sharing in your Remote app to find and control iTunes libraries and Apple TVs that also have Home Sharing turned on.

On your device's Home screen, tap Remote to open the app. Tap Settings. On the Settings screen (see Figure 11.3), tap the button in the Home Sharing section to change it from Off to On. Apple asks you to sign in to your iTunes Store account; type in the Apple ID and password you use for the computers linked by Home Sharing, and then click Done.

Apple verifies your account information and turns on Home Sharing. Now you can use Remote to control any library or Apple TV that participates in Home Sharing.

Using Remote to Control iTunes

After you've set up the Remote app with one or more of your iTunes libraries, you use it to control iTunes in the same way you would play music on your iPod or other portable device. Instead of playing on your device, however, the music or videos plays in iTunes or via Apple TV.

Your computer or TV must be turned on—and with iTunes or Apple TV running—for you to use the Remote app to control them.

If you want to change your settings in Remote, click the Settings button and take one of these actions:

- **Choose a different library**—Remote displays available libraries at the top of the Settings screen. Tap the one you want to gain remote access to it.

- **Add a new library**—Tap Add an iTunes Library and follow the steps listed earlier to add another library to Remote.

- **Delete a library**—Tap the upper-left Edit button. A red Delete icon appears next to each library on your list. Tap that icon and then tap the Delete button to confirm. Click Done when you're finished.

- **Turn Home Sharing on or off**—In the Home Sharing section, tap the On or Off button to enable or disable Home Sharing. If you're turning on Home Sharing, you must enter the Apple ID and password you use for Home Sharing to complete the process.

Copying Files to and from Your Device

You can use your iPad, iPod Touch, or iPhone (running iOS 4 or higher) to share files, transferring copies from your computer to your device or from the device to your computer. You might transfer written notes, other documents, ringtones, and so on.

Connect your device to your computer, select it from the Source list, and click Apps. Scroll down to the File Sharing section, shown in Figure 11.5. (If you don't see this section, you don't have any apps installed that can share files.)

In the File Sharing section, you can move copies of files between your device and your computer:

- **To transfer a file from your device to your computer**—From the Apps list on the left, select an app to see its files. Select the file you want to copy to your computer, and then click Save To. In the dialog box that opens, navigate to where you want to save the file. Select the folder you want and click OK.

- **To transfer a file from your computer to your device**—Select the app that will store your file. Click Add. Find and select the file you want to transfer; click Open.

iTunes syncs with your device and transfers the file.

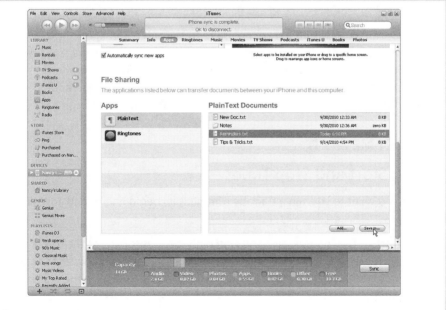

Figure 11.5   *Sharing files via iTunes*

Modifying Tracks

You may have tracks in your library whose length you would like to change. For example, you might want to cut lengthy credits from the beginning of a movie or skip the question-and-answer session at the end of a podcast. Or maybe you want to import a digital recording you made of an old LP or cassette, but the recording is a single long file and you want to make each song its own track.

If you're seriously into editing audio and video files, you should look into a program that's designed to do that (listen to this chapter's Tell Me More file for some suggestions). But you can do some quick-and-dirty track modification right in iTunes.

 SHOW ME   Media 11.3—Changing the Length of a Track
Access this video file through your registered Web Edition at
my.safaribooksonline.com/9780132660273/media.

 TELL ME MORE   Media 11.4—Editing Audio Tracks
Access this audio recording through your registered Web Edition at
my.safaribooksonline.com/9780132660273/media.

Choosing Where a Track Begins and Ends

You may not always want to hear an entire track from beginning to end. For example, if you're listening to songs from a live concert, you may not want to hear the patter at the start of a song or the cheering at the end. iTunes lets you set the beginning and ending points of an item—including songs, videos, audiobooks, and podcasts—so you can skip whatever you don't want at the beginning or end.

 LET ME TRY IT

Setting Start and Stop Times

When you want to shorten a track by trimming its beginning or end, follow these steps:

1. Start by playing the track and watching the Status pane at the top of the iTunes screen. When the track reaches the point where you want to start (or end) it, make a note of the elapsed time that appears in the Status pane.

2. Select the track you want to modify.

3. Select File, Get Info.

4. Click Options to open the Options tab, shown in Figure 11.6.

5a. If you want to trim the beginning of the song, type your desired starting time into the Start Time text box.

5b. If you want to trim the end of the song, type your desired ending time into the Stop Time text box.

6. Click OK.

Now when you play the track, iTunes plays only the portion between the Start Time and Stop Time you indicated.

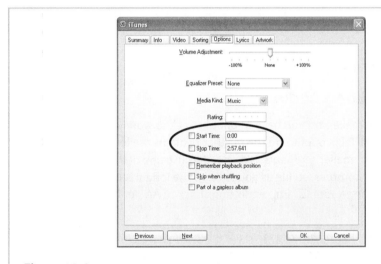

Figure 11.6 *Setting a track's start and stop times*

iTunes doesn't discard any part of the file you trimmed. The whole file is still there; iTunes simply starts or stops playing it at the time marker you specified. If you want to reset the track to its previous length, select the track and select File, Get Info. If you're not sure how long the full-length track is supposed to be, click the Summary tab and look for the track's length, next to its name. (Alternatively, you can check the Time column in List view, which shows the track's full length.)

Click Options and set the Start Time to 0:00 and the Stop Time to the song's length. Click OK. iTunes goes back to playing the entire track.

When you're restoring a track to its full length, you don't have to enter its exact Stop Time. As long as the Stop Time you enter is *longer* than the track's length, iTunes changes the Stop Time to the time at which the track actually finishes. So, for example, if the full length of a song you've trimmed is 2:58:004 and you enter 3:00 in the Stop Time box, iTunes automatically changes that 3:00 to 2:58:004 when you click OK.

Breaking a Long Track into Multiple Shorter Tracks

You can break up one long track into shorter tracks in iTunes. If you primarily get your music from the iTunes Store or by ripping your CD collection, you probably won't run into this situation too often. But you may have a digital recording of a lecture that you want to break into smaller segments, for example, or maybe you're digitizing an old LP.

  LET ME TRY IT

Splitting Up a Long Audio Track

Before you begin, make sure you have a suitable track to work with. Use the iTunes WAV Encoder or AIFF Encoder to rip the CD that contains the long track that you want to break into smaller segments. (You need to use one of these formats so you can work on an uncompressed file as you split up the long track.) After you've ripped the CD, change your CD import settings back to AAC or MP3—whichever you normally use.

Ⓖ *To read about selecting an encoder to use when you import tracks from a CD, **see** "Fine-Tuning CD Import Settings" (in Chapter 2, "Getting Content into iTunes").*

Play the long track you've imported. For each segment you want to create, note the elapsed time of its beginning and ending. When you've written those down, follow these steps:

1. Select the track you want to break up.

2. Choose File, Get Info.

3. Click the Options tab (see Figure 11.6).

4. Type in the Start Time and Stop Time that correspond to the track length you want.

5. Click OK.

6. With the long track selected, choose Advanced, Create AAC Version or Advanced, Create MP3 Version (what you see on the menu depends on the kind of encoder you've chosen in your Import Settings).

7. iTunes creates a new track in the format you chose, using only the segment you've defined. Select the newly created track and click its name. When the name changes to a text box, type in a new name for the track. If you're breaking up one long track containing different songs, for example, type in the name of the song you just split off.

8. Repeat steps 1–7 for each segment that you're turning into a separate track.

9. When you've finished, delete the long track you broke up: Select the track and press the Delete or Backspace key. If prompted, click Remove to confirm that you want to delete the track, and then click Move to Recycle Bin or Move to Trash.

Now you can group the tracks together on a playlist if you want to hear them in order.

Ⓖ *To read about setting up a playlist, **see** "Creating a Playlist" (in Chapter 5).*

Using iTunes Keyboard Shortcuts

As anyone who works with computers can tell you, the fastest, most efficient way to get things done is to use keyboard shortcuts whenever they're available. Instead of reaching for the mouse, moving it around, clicking, and then repositioning your hand on the keyboard, you keep your fingers on the keys—and your mind focused on what you're doing.

iTunes offers keyboard shortcuts for the program's most common activities. This section shows you how to power up your iTunes use with these shortcuts.

Shortcuts for Listening or Watching

When you're listening to music or watching a video in iTunes, you can use keyboard shortcuts to give iTunes instructions, such as to change the volume or move to the next item. Table 11.1 shows you these shortcuts.

Table 11.1   Keyboard Shortcuts to Use While Listening or Watching in iTunes

Action	Windows Keyboard Shortcut	Mac Keyboard Shortcut
Play the selected item	Enter	Return
Stop (or start) playing the selected item	Spacebar	Spacebar
Show the currently playing song	Ctrl+L	Cmd-L
Jump from the currently playing item to the next one in a list	Right arrow	Cmd–Right arrow
Jump from the currently playing item to the previous one in a list	Left arrow	Cmd–Left arrow
Jump to the next album or video in a list	Ctrl+Shift+Alt+Right arrow	Option–Right arrow
Jump to the previous album or video in a list	Ctrl+Shift+Alt+Left arrow	Option–Left arrow
Jump to the next chapter of an audiobook	Ctrl+Shift+Right arrow	Cmd–Shift–Right arrow
Jump to the previous chapter of an audiobook	Ctrl+Shift+Left arrow	Cmd–Shift–Left arrow
Increase volume	Ctrl+Up arrow	Cmd–Up arrow
Decrease volume	Ctrl+Down arrow	Cmd–Down arrow
Mute	Ctrl+Shift+Down arrow	Option–Cmd–Down arrow
Switch to the Mini Player	Ctrl+M	Cmd-M
Display or hide the Visualizer	Ctrl+T	Cmd-T
Toggle full-screen mode on or off while the Visualizer is displayed	Ctrl+F	Cmd-F
Show Visualizer options while the Visualizer is displayed	Question mark (?)	Question mark (?)
Show or hide the Equalizer	Ctrl+Shift+2	Cmd-2

Shortcuts for Working with Your Library

For just about any action you do in your iTunes library—tagging tracks, importing music, browsing your library, adjusting your iTunes preferences, and more—there are keyboard shortcuts to help you out. Table 11.2 lists shortcuts you can use while working with your library.

Table 11.2 Keyboard Shortcuts to Use in Your iTunes Library

Action	Windows Keyboard Shortcut	Mac Keyboard Shortcut
Check or uncheck all items in a list	Ctrl+click the check box next to any item on the list	Cmd–click the check box next to any item on the list
Select all items in a list	Ctrl+A	Cmd-A
Deselect all items in a list	Ctrl+Shift+A	Shift-Cmd-A
Copy the selected item's information or artwork	Ctrl+C	Cmd-C
Cut the selected item's information or artwork	Ctrl+X	Cmd-X
Paste information or artwork from the Clipboard	Ctrl+V	Cmd-V
Add a file to your library	Ctrl+O	Cmd-O
Import a song, playlist, or other file	Ctrl+Shift+O	Shift-Cmd-O
View library in List view	Ctrl+Shift+3	Cmd-3
View library in Album List view	Ctrl+Shift+4	Cmd-4
View library in Grid view	Ctrl+Shift+5	Cmd-5
View library in Cover Flow view	Ctrl+Shift+6	Cmd-6
Show or hide the Artist and Album columns	Ctrl+B	Cmd-B
Show or hide a song's artwork	Ctrl+G	Cmd-G
Open View Options (to select columns to display)	Ctrl+J	Cmd-J
Open iTunes Preferences	Ctrl+Comma (,)	Cmd-Comma (,)
Open Info for the selected item	Ctrl+I	Cmd-I
Delete the selected item from your library and all playlists	Shift+Delete	Option-Delete

Shortcuts for Working with Playlists

Creating playlists can take a lot of work. Table 11.3 makes it easier by listing the keyboard shortcuts that speed up playlist-related tasks.

Table 11.3   Keyboard Shortcuts to Use with Playlists

Action	Windows Keyboard Shortcut	Mac Keyboard Shortcut
Create a new playlist	Ctrl+N	Cmd-N
Create a new playlist using the selected songs	Ctrl+Shift+N	Shift-Cmd-N
Create a new smart playlist	Ctrl+Alt+N	Option-Cmd-N
Delete the selected playlist and all its songs from your library	Shift+Delete	Option-Delete
Delete the selected playlist without confirming that you want to delete it (This does not delete the playlist's individual songs from your library.)	Ctrl+Delete	Cmd-Delete

Shortcuts for Miscellaneous Actions

Table 11.4 lists other actions you can accomplish with keyboard shortcuts while working with iTunes or shopping in the iTunes Store.

Table 11.4   Miscellaneous Keyboard Shortcuts

Action	Windows Keyboard Shortcut	Mac Keyboard Shortcut
Undo your last action	Ctrl+Z	Cmd-Z
Show or hide the iTunes sidebar	Ctrl+Shift+G	Cmd-Shift-G
Eject a CD	Ctrl+E	Cmd-E
Go to the next page in the iTunes Store	Ctrl+Right bracket (])	Cmd–Right bracket (])
Go to the previous page in the iTunes Store	Ctrl+Left bracket ([)	Cmd–Left bracket ([)
Enter an audio file URL to stream to iTunes	Ctrl+U	Cmd-U
Connect device to computer without autosyncing	Connect your device and press Ctrl+Shift+Alt (Hold down the keys until you see your device listed in the iTunes Source list.)	Connect your device and press Cmd-Option (Hold down the keys until you see your device listed in the iTunes Source list.)
Close iTunes	Ctrl+W	Cmd-W

Troubleshooting Tips

Most people find iTunes easy to install and use. But problems do pop up. If you're having difficulty getting iTunes to work the way it's supposed to—for example, you can't connect to the iTunes Store or sync your device—try some of the tips listed in this section.

> Before you troubleshoot iTunes, back up your library! You don't want your media files to disappear with any changes you make to iTunes. Chapter 9 tells you how to back up your entire iTunes library.

Here's a list of possible fixes to common iTunes problems:

- **Run iTunes Diagnostics**—iTunes has a wizard that checks for problems with your computer that may be interfering with iTunes' ability to work properly. In iTunes, select Help, Run Diagnostics to open the wizard, shown in Figure 11.7. Make sure there's a check in the check box of each test you want iTunes to run:
  - **Network connectivity tests**—These tests check two things: the hardware and software your system uses to connect to a network, and whether your computer can connect to the Internet and establish a secure connection with the iTunes Store.
  - **CD/DVD drive tests**—You need to insert a disc that contains data (such as an audio CD) to test your CD/DVD drive. These tests check your computer's optical drive, the drive where you insert CDs or DVDs, looking to see whether the device's driver is installed correctly and whether it can read a disc inserted in the drive.
  - **Device connectivity tests**—These tests check your computer's USB port and whether your computer can recognize and connect to your iPod or other portable device.
  - **Device sync tests**—If you're having trouble syncing your portable device with iTunes, run these tests, which check necessary software and run a test sync.

Click OK to have iTunes check your system for problems. iTunes returns a report that lists the tests it ran. A green light next to a test means that the test found no problem. A yellow light indicates a possible problem, and a red light means the test failed. Click the Help button next to a failed test for more information about the problem.

iTunes Diagnostics tests don't solve any problems that your computer may be having. Instead, they look for and identify common issues so that you can take steps to correct them.

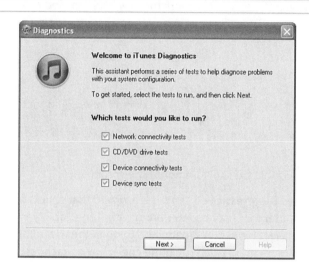

Figure 11.7 *iTunes Diagnostics*

- **Make sure you have the latest version of iTunes**—In iTunes, select Help, Check for Updates and install any updates that are available.

- **Make sure your device is up-to-date**—You can check for updates to your device's software via iTunes. Connect the device to your computer and select it in the Source list. On the device's Summary page, click the Check for Updates button. (Your device automatically checks for updates periodically, but you can double-check using this method.)

- **Restore your device's original settings**—If you're having trouble with your device and an update doesn't help, you might want to try restoring its original settings. Restoring resets your device to its original, factory settings and deletes any information you've added to the device. Connect the device to your computer and select it in the Source list. On the device's Summary page, click Restore. iTunes backs up your device and restores its original settings. When it's finished, you can restore backed-up settings, notes, contacts, calendars, and so on by right-clicking your device in the Source list and selecting Restore from Backup.

It's a good idea to back up your device at least once a month—once a week is even better. Hang on to the last two or three backups. That way, if you need to restore your device, you can choose which backup to use.

- **Check for viruses**—Make sure your antivirus software is up-to-date. Then disconnect from the Internet and run a virus scan. If your antivirus program finds any viruses, malware, or other suspicious files, follow its recommendations to remove or quarantine them. Then reconnect to the Internet and try using iTunes again.

- **Create a new iTunes library**—If the new library works, try importing the files from the old library.

  Ⓖ *See* "Creating Multiple Libraries" (in Chapter 8, "Managing Your iTunes Library") to learn how to create a new iTunes library.

- **Windows users: Disable Direct X**—If you use Windows XP, Vista, or 7 and you're having trouble watching video, try disabling Direct X acceleration in QuickTime. Open QuickTime and select Edit, Preferences, QuickTime Preferences. Click the Advanced tab, shown in Figure 11.8. In the Video section, select Safe Mode (GDI Only). Click OK, and try playing a video in iTunes.

- **Reinstall iTunes and QuickTime**—Sometimes you can solve the problem by reinstalling the software.

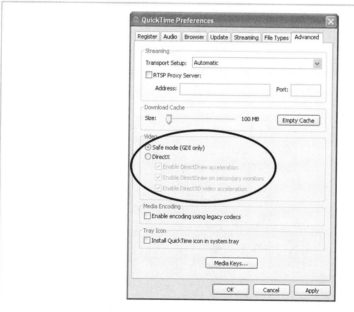

Figure 11.8   *Disabling DirectX in QuickTime*

Apple Support has many help options when you're having trouble getting iTunes to work properly. Go to www.apple.com/support and type a keyword related to your problem into the upper-right search box to find possible answers. Or click Communities to visit the Apple forums, where you can ask a question and get answers from experienced iTunes users.

index

W-X-Y-Z